The Genovese Mafia Family

The Complete History of New York Crime Organization

Mafia Library

© Copyright 2022 Mafia Library - All rights reserved.

The content contained within this book may not be reproduced, duplicated or transmitted without direct written permission from the author or the publisher.

Under no circumstances will any blame or legal responsibility be held against the publisher, or author, for any damages, reparation, or monetary loss due to the information contained within this book, either directly or indirectly.

Legal Notice:

This book is copyright protected. It is only for personal use. You cannot amend, distribute, sell, use, quote or paraphrase any part, or the content within this book, without the consent of the author or publisher.

Disclaimer Notice:

Please note the information contained within this document is for educational and entertainment purposes only. All effort has been executed to present accurate, up to date, reliable, complete information. No warranties of any kind are declared or implied. Readers acknowledge that the author is not engaged in the rendering of legal, financial, medical or professional advice. The content within this book has been derived from various sources. Please consult a licensed professional before attempting any techniques outlined in this book.

By reading this document, the reader agrees that under no circumstances is the author responsible for any losses, direct or indirect, that are incurred as a result of the use of the information contained within this document, including, but not limited to, errors, omissions, or inaccuracies.

Table of Contents

INTRODUCTION 1

CHAPTER 1: *LA COSA NOSTRA* 5
    SICILIAN ROOTS 5
    OMERTA 7
    LABOR AND THE MAFIA 9
    HIERARCHY 11

CHAPTER 2: THE EARLY YEARS 15
    THE 107TH STREET MOB 15
    ALLIANCE AND ARREST 16
    THE MAFIA-CAMORRA WAR 18
    PROHIBITION AND THE CASTELLAMMARESE WAR 22

CHAPTER 3: THE LUCIANO ERA 27
    THE FIVE FAMILIES 27
    THE COMMISSION 31
    LUCK RUNS OUT 36

CHAPTER 4: DON VITO 43
    THE NEAPOLITAN DON 43
    EXILE 49
    RETURN TO NEW YORK 55
    CAUGHT AT LAST 62

CHAPTER 5: THE ROAD TO THE RICO ACT 65
    THE VALACHI HEARINGS AND THE END OF *OMERTA* 65
    THE CRUSADERS 66
    THE ERA OF "FRONT BOSSES" 68
    THE RICO ACT 69

CHAPTER 6: VINCENT "THE CHIN" GIGANTE AND THE 1980S 71
    EXPANSION 71
    VINCENT "THE CHIN" GIGANTE 73
    RUDY GIULIANI AND THE MAFIA TRIALS 75
    THE DOWNFALL OF GIGANTE 77

CHAPTER 7: MAFIA IN THE NEW MILLENNIUM 81
  THE CHIN IN PRISON 81
  THE FINAL CRACKDOWN 83
  THE GENOVESE FAMILY TODAY 85

CONCLUSION 89

REFERENCES 93

Introduction

In 1972, the release of Francis Ford Coppola's film *The Godfather* brought the concept of the American Mafia rushing back into the collective American consciousness. A romanticized yet brutal portrayal of this Italian-American criminal subculture, *The Godfather* is indeed what most people think of when they hear the word "Mafia." Since its release, a steady stream of Mafia-based media has met continuing and reliable success, proving the impact that the concept of the American Mafia has had on the broader American culture. From *Goodfellas* to *The Sopranos*, *Donnie Brasco* to *Casino*, *The Untouchables* to *The Irishman*, Mafia life appears to be one of the surest recipes for success in cinema. Put simply, millions of people around the world are fascinated by Mafia-style organized crime

It is true that what most people know about the Mafia is what is communicated on screen, in dramatized retellings of stories which can vary from faithful adaptations to complete works of fiction. But what is the Mafia outside of its screen portrayals? What have they done to garner such international attention and interest? How did the Mafia become so immensely powerful so as to prompt a concerted effort by law enforcement to eradicate the Italian-American subculture completely? Most importantly, how did the Mafia actually work? Perhaps the best way to answer these questions, and to examine possibly the most influential of American criminal cultures, is to examine what is possibly the most influential of organizations within it—the Genovese Crime Family.

The Genovese Family, named for the famed Neapolitan gangster Vito Genovese, is one of the oldest Mafia crime families in the United States. The modern family can trace their roots all the way back to one of the first known mafiosi (members of the Mafia) to immigrate from the old country: The Sicilian mobster Giuseppe "Clutch Hand" Morello. From their humble origins as the small-time 107th Street Mob in East Harlem, Morello was the first in a line of legendary Mafia bosses to control the Genovese Family, including Charles "Lucky" Luciano, Vincent "The Chin" Gigante, and Vito Genovese himself. Since the 1890s, the organization has climbed its way to the heights of the criminal underworld, and has earned its reputation as one of the most formidable and enduring forces in organized crime. Today, the Genovese Family represents roughly one-fifth of New York's Mafia presence and is one of the infamous "Five Families of New York," the others being the Lucchese, Bonanno, Gambino, and Colombo Families. Despite the massive crackdown on organized crime that the United States has seen over the past several decades, the Genovese Family remains arguably the most powerful American crime organization to this day.

Vito Genovese himself, the namesake of the organization, was instrumental in cementing the Family's place at the top of the criminal hierarchy. Born just north of the southern Italian city of Napoli ("Naples" in English), Vito immigrated with his family to the United States when he was just 15, settling in the Italian community of Little Italy in New York City. Beginning his career as a small-time criminal and petty thief, Vito eventually found himself in the company of fellow rising gangsters Lucky Luciano and Frank Costello, two individuals who will figure prominently in the story of the Genovese Family. The three men had begun working for a powerful local boss, Joe Masseria (who at the time happened to be in control of the organization which would one day bear Vito's name) and took part in the famous and pivotal Castellammarese War, a conflict which would result in long term changes to the Mafia world landscape.

By the time Vito took control of Giuseppe Morello's former gang, he had already established himself as a ruthless leader who commanded the respect of those around him. But aside from this, Vito also led an incredibly interesting life. From his beginning as a local crook to his ascent to second-in-command to the legendary Lucky Luciano to becoming boss himself, Vito Genovese proved to be an incredibly opportunistic criminal, looking to make an illicit income wherever it could be found. Fleeing the country during the second World War to avoid indictment, Vito found himself making profits allying himself with both sides of the war, the Axis, and later, the Allies. Extradited back to the United States, Vito once again escaped prosecution and retook control of his family, only to follow in the footsteps of so many Mafia bosses before and after him—he was caught, convicted, and sent to prison where he would spend the rest of his days. Though the man is gone, the modern family still bears his name, a testament to the lasting impact of Vito Genovese's legacy on the Italian-American Mafia subculture.

So, the cause for focusing closely on the Genovese Family is clear enough. However, the question remains: Why do we find the concept of the Mafia so interesting in the first place? The credit certainly does not lie in the merits and deeds of Vito Genovese himself, nor his organization. In large part, to answer this question we must return to the beginning of this introduction. Nineteen seventy-twos *The Godfather* and its sequels present eager audiences with a dramatic and highly theatrical tale of the American Mafia. These films took the principle of the Mafia's moral "code of honor" to its romantic extreme and in doing so, they present a tantalizing and intriguing view of organized crime, one which is both accurate and fictitious. While the so-called Mafia code of honor did exist, we find that it is highly flexible and generally absent on a practical level—when it comes to cutthroat crime organizations, there is often very little room for morality and loyalty, as will be seen in later chapters. Although the concept of loyalty was glorified within Mafia culture, backstabbing and betrayal became some of the main running themes of Mafia style organized crime. Aside from cinema, the fact is that any complex organization that became so disproportionately powerful, with its dramatic traditionalism and tendency toward sensational crimes, would become a topic of mass interest. And so we must now ask: How did the Mafia come to occupy this space?

The concept of the Mafia is complex, yet not difficult to understand. Working on a strict code of silence, the Mafia operated underground for decades. Through its formative years, Families came to be organized under clearly defined hierarchies and ranks, from the "Boss of Bosses" down to the lowly associates. These associates, who were not "Made Men" and thus not protected under Mafia structures, nonetheless often made up the bulk of a given Family's workforce, and often included non-Italians who, according to the code, could not officially become members of a Mafia Family. These organizations engaged in a variety of crimes, including extortion, robbery, prostitution, gambling, drug running, trafficking, labor racketeering, smuggling, and more. Being opportunistic by nature, Mafia organizations would generally pursue all routes of income in illicit markets. Prohibition, for example, only opened up new markets for organized crime to manufacture, smuggle, and peddle high demand goods. The introduction of legalized casinos presented similarly promising opportunities, especially for the Genovese Family. And although some were averse to the distribution of narcotics, the Mafia was nevertheless instrumental in establishing the international illicit drug trade. These power structures, along with their willingness to dabble in taboo markets, ensured that Mafia style organized crime would be a persistent force in the American underworld.

In short, the story of the American Mafia is one worth learning. Finding their roots in rural Sicily, American Families often began as loose organizations of immigrants from particular regions of Italy (the "Mafia" from Sicily, the "Camorra" from Campania, the "'Ndrangheta" from Calabria, etc.). In the American context, it was often a means to obtain economic and social security in a time of considerable anti-Italian bigotry. Eventually coming to monopolize certain illegal markets and becoming powerful enough to hold political sway, the United States government eventually undertook to eliminate Italian-American organized crime completely. Through an aggressive campaign of espionage and witness recruiting, the American Mafia was decimated and turned into a shell of its former self. Yet it persists to this day, including the most powerful of its organizations, founded by Giuseppe Morello before the dawn of the twentieth century. This book will detail the rise of the Genovese Family, their peak of notoriety under the rule of Don Vito, and their journey through the margins of American life.

Chapter 1:

La Cosa Nostra

Before beginning the history of the Genovese Family in particular, it is helpful to first understand the concept and origins of the Mafia in general. To do this, we must go all the way back to 19th century southern Italy, where the first loose organizations of Sicilians which would come to be known as "the Mafia" began to take shape. Originally meant to serve a genuine social function in a time of turmoil, these organizations would eventually grow into international enterprises, completely unrecognizable from their infant forms. The moral codes which the modern American Mafia claims to operate under are drawn from the Mafia's roots in the old country, as is the strict hierarchy which was developed to maintain a chain of command within its structures. These concepts are key to understanding the functioning of the Genovese Family, and this chapter will explain the foundations, origins, codes, and structures of these organizations.

Sicilian Roots

Being a highly secretive organization which was not in the business of keeping records of their activities, the origins of the Mafia in Sicily are difficult to trace. However, there is a great deal that can be gleaned from what we do know about the Mafia's earliest days, and this can paint a clear enough picture of what kind of organization we are dealing with. After Sicily became a part of Italy in the 19th century, the small island faced a period of social upheaval. Land redistribution, the elimination of certain traditional customs, and the introduction of capitalist structures resulted in a drastically altered way of life in Sicily. An increase in private property inevitably resulted in an increase of petty crime and thievery, made worse by the notable lack of official law enforcement on the island.

Realizing that the new federal government would be offering little support to curb the rise of property crime, local elites who had already been accustomed to relying on privately hired security and guardsmen began enlisting men (many of whom had themselves been criminals) to serve as a kind of pseudo-vigilante group. Meant to prevent and remedy various property crimes and disputes, these groups, almost exclusively found in the western portion of the island, have often been referred to as the "proto-Mafia" by prominent Mafia scholars such as Salvatore Lupo. Generally, the leaders of these vigilante groups were entitled to extract a certain portion of whatever goods they managed to recover—an obvious precursor to Mafia style extortion tactics. So, somewhat ironically, the Mafia very likely began as a substitute for official law enforcement. In the aftermath of the official abolition of the feudal land system, these "proto-Mafia" groups came to represent western Sicily's retention of their feudal past.

Even before the Mafia was a publicly known phenomenon, it was a commonly understood fact of life that in western Sicily, being successful meant being connected to criminals: "There was no alternative: In order to defend oneself and one's property, one was obliged to seek the patronage of robbers" (Lupo, 2009). The term "Mafia" first came into prominence around 1860 (the term Camorra, later used to describe Neapolitan organized crime organizations, was considerably older). The first time it was mentioned in a police report was soon after, referring to an organization run by Antonino Giammona in the city of Palermo in the 1870s. Giammona, like most top Sicilian mafiosi, had been involved in politics. This is another tradition carried over into the Mafia's American incarnation—that is, criminal overlords who seek out and maintain connections in the political as well as illicit realms. After 1860, the federal Italian government used Mafia members extensively in their strict, authoritarian rule of the island.

It is a subject of debate whether or not the American Mafia should even be considered an extension of these Sicilian organizations or if they should be seen as a wholly separate entity. Given the fact that much of the immigration from Italy to the United States and Canada came from the crime-riddled western portion of Sicily, and considering the high degree of traditionalism, there is reason to believe that the American Mafia, at least, views itself as an outgrowth of their Sicilian ancestors. Although many early mafiosi immigrated to North America prior to the beginning of the 20th century, one of the largest periods of immigration was during the 1920s. This happened to coincide with the rise of Fascism in Italy, and during the mid-to-late 1920s, a massive crackdown of Mafia activity on the island took place under the Fascist, dictatorial prefect Cesare Mori. The first (and certainly not last) large-scale attempt to eradicate the Mafia took place in this period, and it drove hundreds of known mafiosi out of their home country. Many were destined for New York City.

However Giuseppe Morello, with whom the story of the Genovese Family begins, found himself at home in New York decades earlier. Sometime in the early 1890s, Morello had emigrated from his hometown of Corleone, Sicily (interestingly, this is the same birthplace as *The Godfather*'s iconic Don Vito Corleone, formerly Andolini), likely to escape prosecution for his past Mafia activity. Already a seasoned criminal, Morello is possibly the first known Sicilian mafioso to carry his outlaw past over to "set up shop" in New York City. Having established the foundations of the Genovese Family, being imprisoned, and being forced into exile, Morello remained a lifelong criminal until his past finally caught up with him. The legendary Sicilian gangster was gunned down in 1930.

Omerta

The origins of the term *omerta*, also referred to as the Mafia "code of silence," are not perfectly clear. Though, there are clues to be found in how the term is used. Generally, *omerta* can refer to the Mafia itself, to a code of traditionalist morality that mafiosi sometimes claim to be guided by, or simply to the act of not divulging the existence of the Mafia and its structures. One theory claims that the word is derived from the Italian word "uomo," meaning "man." We can assume, then, that *omerta* refers to being a man, to possessing qualities of manliness or *machismo*, or by being a part of a brotherhood of men. It can also refer to a man who handles his own problems, one who settles scores on his own terms, without appealing to a higher, state level authority, such as the government or the police. There is merit here, as this does directly relate to the concept of *omerta* as we know it—the disdain for law enforcement and the desire to keep all Mafia related issues "in the family." According to *omerta*, the Mafia's activities, successes, and problems are no one's business but the Mafia's. This includes the state.

Another theory suggests that *omerta* is chiefly derived from the Italian word for "humility." This also makes good sense. *Umilta*, when spoken with a Sicilian dialect that often replaces "l" sounds with "r" sounds, sounds terribly close to *omerta*. Those with *umilta* showed respect and reverence for the group to which they belonged, understanding that some degree of self-sacrifice may be necessary for the betterment of the larger clan. They do not act in such a way so as to harm the group or fellow members, which necessitates a general distrust toward outsiders.

This definition fits perfectly with the core tenet of the Mafia: Utter silence toward all those who are not within *La Cosa Nostra* (literally, "our thing," or "the thing of ours"). This *omerta* or *umilta* is the main reason for the difficulty in studying the Mafia, and has been a thorn in the sides of historians (and law enforcement) for decades, as breaching *omerta* was considered a serious offense. Even after the Valachi hearings of 1963 publicly exposed the Mafia, many traditionalist mafiosi held true to their code of silence. As late as 1985, when high ranking gangster Gaetano Badalamenti faced trial and imprisonment in the famous "Pizza Connection" drug ring trials, he refused to expose sensitive details, even to his own attorney: "I have never betrayed and I will never betray my secrets" (Lupo, 2015).

However, even some of the most respected and high ranking mafiosi had been known to break *omerta*. Joseph Bonanno, boss of the family that bears his name even today, had been exposed for cooperating with law enforcement in Italy in the 1930s. Both Vito Genovese and Lucky Luciano had at one point been enlisted by government agents. And, since lowly Genovese soldier Joe Valachi's explosive 1963 testimony, the Mafia has seen a steady stream of mafiosi-turned-witnesses. The point is that, even in a culture as traditionalist and conservative as the Mafia, no code of honor is unbreakable when one's own self-interest is too great. The fact is that *omerta* more so represented a utopian, idealized version of what a mafioso should be, a paragon to be aspired to, rather than a realistic representation of everyday Mafia behavior and culture.

Along with the code of silence, *omerta* can also refer to the Mafia's history of tradition and symbolism. Supposedly old Sicilian ways of communication and representation were carried over into the American Mafia, resulting in an environment where certain symbols came to bear special meaning for mafiosi. Some of the best examples of these come from popular media, but are generally based in fact. For example, *The Godfather*'s "Sicilian message," consisting of a dead fish wrapped in a piece of clothing, meant to signify that that owner of the clothes is now "sleeping with the fishes." In *The Sopranos*, when fictional *capo* Jimmy Altieri was assassinated for spying on behalf of the government, his body was found with a rat stuffed in his mouth, meant to send a clear message to all would-be government informants. Pop culture references to Mafia symbolism abound, but the real life instances of such messages are often even more disturbing. In 1982 when gangster Antonino Inzerillo was found murdered, he had a single $5 bill stuffed in his mouth, and another two on his genitals. Markers like these functioned as messages to other potential violators and as a way of communicating why the murder took place. In this case, Inzerillo clearly had a big mouth, and was far too greedy for his own good.

Labor and the Mafia

Understanding the dynamics of labor and unionism is key to understanding how Mafia organizations operate. In this context, labor is seen as a commodity from which profit can be extracted. It is something that can be manipulated, and unions proved to be an effective tool with which corrupt Mafia associated officials could use to leverage labor power to their advantage. Mafia groups have been known to use unions from both sides—organizing strikes and work stoppages in some cases, orchestrating violent strikebreaks in others.

Indeed, labor unionism has historically been one of the strongest pillars of Mafia income.

Mafia organizations have seemingly been involved in some degree of labor control from the inception. In Mafia controlled regions of Sicily during their formative years, the most valuable export to be found was sulfur, which was extracted from various mining operations. These mining operations became increasingly intertwined with Mafia structures throughout the 19th century, when the trade in sulfur was booming and Sicily controlled a vast portion of the market. This is what Lupo refers to as the Mafia's tendency toward "popular associationism" (2009), which refers to Mafia organizations' general desire to become entangled with existing public and private institutions. This phenomenon was present even before labor unionism became a lucrative sector for organized crime.

One prominent example is Don Giuseppe Lumia, who owned and operated a sulfur mine in Caltanissetta. Running his mine in a way that is reflective of the form Mafia structures would eventually take, Lumia was eventually murdered by disgruntled workers over a wage dispute. Disputes like these would become common in the era of Mafia unionism. In a move that foreshadows the Mafia's use of symbolism, Lumia's murderers left a message on his body indicating that his greed was the cause of his death. In another case, the workforce of a sulfur mine in Favara was dominated by members of a *Fratellanza* (brotherhood), which was eventually placed under investigation and designated as a Mafia Family in the mid-1880s.

When Mafia structures were eventually transplanted from the old world to the United States, many of their practices came with them, including labor control. Beginning in the 1930s during the American labor movement, labor and union racketeering had grown to become one of the most reliable income sources for Mafia organizations. Extortion from both businesses and workers was commonplace, and these practices thrived for decades before any serious attention was paid. Although Robert Kennedy had made labor racketeering a priority since 1961 when he became attorney general, no concerted, national effort was made until the assassination of infamous labor leader Jimmy Hoffa in 1975. Hoffa will come up again later in this story, however it is important now to understand his connection to the Teamsters union, now famous for its history of Mafia corruption. Viewing Mafia involvement in unions as something that extorted and burglarized workers, and as something that threatened society itself, the United States undertook to reform the practice of labor unionism.

Labor racketeering is perhaps one of the most cynical Mafia activities in its history. Something originally meant to empower workers and improve the lives of society's most vulnerable was hijacked and opportunistically devoured by the American Mafia. The extent of Mafia involvement in unionism up until the 1980s was intense, and to this day, no other country has had a union system as corrupt as that of the United States.

Hierarchy

Mafia Families generally operate under a strict hierarchy of ranks. As the name *La Cosa Nostra* ("our thing") suggests, the Mafia is inherently exclusive. Being within it brings many advantages and prestige. Being on the outside means being generally kept out of the loop and being viewed with far more distrust than a member would normally express toward another member. Individuals involved with a Family but who are not Made Men are generally referred to as "associates." These associates would often do grunt work and the dirtier jobs, and were generally organized as groups or "crews" under the command of a higher ranking Made Man.

As a general rule, Mafia rankings consist of the following: At the top, the undisputed head of the organization is the boss or don. These are generally the mafiosi that people know best—Lucky Luciano, Joe Bonanno, Vito Genovese, Al Capone, etc. In some cases, Mafia Families will form committees or juntas to govern the family when the boss is incarcerated or otherwise unavailable. Acting bosses were also common, who would fill in as the official replacement for a boss. As will be discussed in later chapters, there were also a number of so-called "front bosses," who were meant to be viewed by law enforcement as the "official" boss, while the true head of the Family operated in secret. Needless to say, being the boss brings unrivaled advantages, but also makes one a massive target, both to law enforcement and fellow power-hungry, backstabbing mafiosi.

Under the boss is the *sottocapo*, or underboss. There was generally only one underboss at a time, and they would be the boss' second-in-command and would govern the *capos*. Typically, Mafia bosses were once underbosses who claimed the position after the prior boss was arrested, retired, or was murdered (sometimes by the underboss himself). In some cases, however, bosses who became incapacitated were sometimes replaced by the *consigliere*. A *consigliere* was a special position within Mafia Families, usually occupied by senior Family figures and were generally the boss' most trusted ally. They served as special advisors and counselors to the boss, and would often represent them in high level meetings which the boss was unable to attend. While even underbosses were sometimes seen with distrust by paranoid bosses, consiglieres were those who had earned the boss' utter confidence. Again, it was *The Godfather* that brought the term *"consigliere"* into the public consciousness with the legendary onscreen Mafia character of Tom Hagen, the most trusted advisor to Don Corleone.

Below the underboss are the *caporegimes*, or *capos*, and soldiers. *Capos* function similarly to military officers, commanding a crew of soldiers. These *capos* serve the function of middle management within Mafia structures. Soldiers are the lowest level of the Mafia "Made" totem pole. That is, they still command respect due to being a "Made Man," but are subservient to *capos*, the underboss, and of course, the Boss. Just as *capos* would run a crew made up of soldiers, soldiers would usually run crews themselves, made up of non-Made associates of the family. While associates are not protected under Mafia rules, being a member of a respected soldier's crew brought many benefits. Individuals in every position would run their own criminal enterprises or would be involved in larger ones organized by higher level members. As a rule, each position would kick up a part of their earnings to their superior. Associates kicked up their profit to their commanding soldier, soldiers to the *capos*, and *capos* to the underboss and boss. The boss would receive a share of all income made within the Family. Withholding earnings was considered a serious offense.

There is one more position that should be discussed, as it will be an important theme in the story. The "Boss of Bosses," was largely an unofficial position, but at certain points in the Mafia's history, bosses of certain Families would declare themselves the head of all Mafia activities. This usually happens when a boss believes that their Family is powerful enough to command the respect of *all other* Mafia bosses and their crews. Two such individuals were Sal Maranzano and Vito Genovese himself. As will be seen, this was far from a permanent position.

Chapter 2:

The Early Years

The unit that today is called the Genovese Family has had several incarnations, been known by several different names, and been led by a diverse cast of interesting characters. This chapter will focus on the earliest manifestation of the Genovese Family, its founder, and the first few decades of the fledgling Mafia criminal organization.

The 107th Street Mob

Born in 1867 near the city of Palermo, Giuseppe Morello was associated with the Sicilian Mafia from an early age, when his widowed mother married a known mafioso in Corleone. His mother and new father's marriage would produce several half-siblings of Morello, three of whom (Vincenzo, Ciro, and Nicolo) would become involved in Morello's early criminal activity. Becoming a bona fide Sicilian mafioso before ever setting foot in the United States, Morello was faced with a crisis in the early 1890s. He was under investigation and was likely to be sentenced for two crimes he was involved in: Murder and producing counterfeit currency.

Morello had become one of the most trusted men under Paolino Streva, a Corleonese Mafia captain. Soon after learning that Sicilian law enforcement was investigating Streva, the lead investigator Giovanni Vella was shot dead. After a witness testified to seeing Morello at the scene of the crime, the witness was also found murdered soon after. With all fingers clearly pointed at Morello, he now feared prosecution. Sometime around 1892-1894, Morello decided to emigrate from Sicily to the United States to avoid sentencing. It is likely that his familial Mafia connections in Corleone assisted in coordinating his escape.

Despite his flight from the country, Morello was officially sentenced in Sicily.

Upon arriving in the United States, along with much of his family, Morello traveled the country in search of work. After a streak of bad luck in Louisiana and in Texas, including failed job opportunities and contracting malaria, Morello moved back to New York City sometime in the latter half of the 1890s. Back in New York, Morello became involved in a few different business projects, the earliest of which were mostly failures. Eventually able to get back on his feet, Morello decided to employ the same business tactics that he learned from his time in the Sicilian Mafia. He formed the 107th Street Mob, based in the Italian neighborhoods in East Harlem, the Bronx, and Manhattan. This grouping was the first incarnation of the Genovese Family, and would go on to be known officially as the Morello Family.

Over the next few years, Morello's mob became involved in several businesses, including a Manhattan pub, barber shops, and shoe stores. However, one of Morello's known nicknames, "The Banker," suggests that he was very likely also involved in predatory lending, otherwise known as loansharking. In addition to this, the Morello Family became involved in robbery, extortion, and of course, counterfeiting. The illegal funds earned through this racketeering were laundered through the legitimate businesses owned by the family, establishing a system of money laundering that would be used by future Mafia families for the next century.

Alliance and Arrest

In 1903, another of Morello's siblings who migrated to the United States, his half-sister Salvatrice, married another influential Mafia boss in Little Italy, the Italian neighborhood of Manhattan. This resulted in an alliance between Morello and his new brother-in-law, Ignazio Lupo. Like Morello, Lupo had fled Sicily for the United States to escape prosecution for Mafia-related crimes. Lupo also came to own a series of legitimate businesses, and also became one of the largest importers of olive oil and citrus fruits from his home country. As it happens, the citrus trade in Sicily, along with sulfur mining, was one of the main pillars of income for the Sicilian Mafia, and it is very likely that Lupo's exporters on the other side were Mafia connections.

Together, Morello and Lupo expanded their counterfeiting business along with their other ventures. They had recruited powerful members into the Family, including such notable names as Joe Masseria and Sal D'Aquila, and had become infamous for their tendency to dispose of their murdered enemies' bodies in wooden barrels. The Family continued to grow and as early as 1905, the Morello Family had become the most powerful and influential of New York's Sicilian organized crime groups. Giuseppe Morello had become the first *capo de tutti capi*—Boss of Bosses. Before this point, however, Morello had a fateful first encounter with an NYPD Lieutenant named Joe Petrosino. Along with fellow gangster Vito Cascio-Ferro, Morello was arrested by Petrosino for suspicion of running a counterfeiting operation. Morello, however, remained a free man.

Years later in 1909, Petrosino was sent to Sicily in order to conduct undercover work and investigate the Mafia connection between Palermo in Sicily and New York in the United States. One of his main goals was to investigate the history of Sicilian immigrants in America to discover potential criminal records in their home country. Under U.S. law at the time, immigrants could be deported from the country if they were found to have committed crimes in another nation. U.S. law enforcement wanted to uncover criminal pasts of individuals in the country who they suspected of being involved in organized crime. As it turns out, Giuseppe Morello was one of those individuals.

Perhaps Petrosino's first mistake was having a fundamental distrust toward the Italian authorities. Petrosino was himself an Italian immigrant, and believing that Italian-American organized crime was a stain on his heritage, he became a kind of crusader against the Mafia. Having a generally cynical attitude, Petrosino believed that Italian authorities were either incompetent or they were in fact directly involved in the Sicilian Mafia—otherwise, it could not have flourished as it did. He refused any state assistance during his brief time in Sicily. His second and more severe mistake was not assuming that his plans may have been known to the very people he was meant to investigate. Likely fearing that Petrosino would discover Morello's compromising criminal past, the Family took action. Morello Family members Antonino Passananti and Carlo Constantino arrived back in their home country of Sicily at almost the exact same time that Petrosino landed. This was not a coincidence. Before anything fruitful could come of Petrosino's investigation, the New York police lieutenant was gunned down in Palermo in March of 1909. Despite the fact that Morello had men in Sicily with Petrosino, it is unknown who his actual assailants were, as Petrosino had made many enemies, and his arrival was clearly less than clandestine.

Although Petrosino was now gone, Morello's time as the most powerful counterfeiter in New York was running short. Both he and his partner Lupo were arrested that same year, in late 1909. A few months later in 1910, the pair were sentenced to 25 and 35 years in prison, respectively. His cousins Fortunato and Tomasso, also known as the Lomonte Brothers, would take control of the family in 1910 in his absence.

The Mafia-Camorra War

Fortunato and Tomasso ran Morello's Family in East Harlem for the first few years of Morello's prison sentence. Fortunato was shot in 1914, and the next year, Tomasso was gunned down as well. Nicolo, Morello's youngest half-brother, would then take control of the family until 1916. Nicolo would end up being murdered during the Mafia-Camorra War, a bloody conflict between Morello's Family and the Camorra, another crime organization originating from the Campania region of Italy.

The Camorra is unique in terms of Italian-American criminal groups. Whereas the Sicilian Mafia organized under a highly stratified and clearly defined leadership hierarchy with a singular Boss who everyone else answered to, the Camorra had a far more loose and decentralized structure. Rather than one shot caller, the Camorra used a kind of clan-based committee decision making system. Because power is more evenly distributed in organizations like the Camorra, they tend to be more stable, as there is less incentive to backstab and scheme to attain a higher rank. The disadvantage is that because of this style or organization, they tend to be less powerful and generally incapable of most of the high level crimes committed by Mafia Families. This is why the vast majority of infamous and high profile burglaries, scams, and assassinations were carried out by nationally powerful Mafia Families, not the Camorra. Structures such as the Mafia can be described as "vertically" organized, whereas the Camorra were "horizontally" organized.

Since the Family had been weakened by Morello and Lupo's imprisonments, there had been a power struggle developing between the Family and the Neapolitan Camorra. At the time, the Camorra was headed by Brooklyn mobsters Andrea Ricci, Alessandro Vollero, and Pellegrino Morano. Vollero and Morano were looking to expand their operations, and looked to the so-called "King of Little Italy," Giosue Gallucci, a prominent *camorrista* businessman with important political connections. Gallucci ran a highly profitable "numbers" racket in the Italian areas of East Harlem, which the Camorra had largely been denied access to. Numbers rackets were essentially a lottery, with gamblers placing bets to predict a set of numbers which would be drawn at random. Bets would usually be collected by the foot soldiers, or "runners," soliciting in the generally poor Italian neighborhoods, or at local businesses owned by the Family and doubling as bookmaking hubs, or "bookies."

In May of 1915, as tensions continued to rise, Giosue Gallucci was murdered by the Camorra. It is alleged that the money for the hit was personally put up by Morano himself. Complicating matters was the fact that Gallucci was, at the time, allied with the Morello Family. A major conflict ensued between the Morellos and the Camorra bosses over control of the late Gallucci's numbers rackets. Initially, however, the Mafia and Camorra were relatively peaceful toward each other. Joe DeMarco, a longtime enemy of the Morellos, became a major impediment to both the Mafia and the Camorra in extending their numbers rackets, as DeMarco controlled much of lower Manhattan's gambling operations.

After the Morellos resolved once again to eliminate DeMarco (they had failed several times prior), the main issue was that DeMarco was familiar with most of Morello's hitmen, and thus it would be difficult to approach him by surprise. Meeting with Camorra men on Coney Island in 1916, the two organizations planned a surprise attack on DeMarco. Joe Verizzano, an associate of the Morellos and an unknown face to DeMarco, was selected to plan the hit. Verizzano was meant to enter one of DeMarco's establishments and gamble. He would point out DeMarco to a *camorrista* hitman who was meant to also be undercover in the building. However, the first attempt on DeMarco's life failed. Persistent, the gangs planned another similar attack, and when the assigned gunman accidentally shot the wrong person, Verizzano murdered DeMarco himself. Now with the Mafia and Camorra's common enemy eliminated, they began to plot against each other. The bloodshed that followed became known as the "Mafia-Camorra War."

The conflict eventually became so intense that it has been said that members of both gangs feared to venture into the other's territory, knowing that it meant a death sentence. After months of bloody fighting, Camorra officials offered the Morello Family a truce. Their goal, however, was not peace. Current Morello boss Nicolo Morello (also known as Nicolo Terranova), and his bodyguard Charles Ubriaco were lured to a meeting with Morano and other Camorra leaders. At this meeting in September of 1916, the pair were gunned down.

Following Nicolo and Ubriaco's assassination, more killings ensued. The Camorra were aggressively pursuing Morello Family members and were able to kill several of them, including DeMarco's assassin, Joe Verizzano. However the Morellos themselves, including Giuseppe's remaining half-siblings, remained close to their home territory and out of the reach of Camorra hitmen. The *camorristas* became more and more brazen in their tactics and behaved recklessly in their pursuit of top level Morello men. Generally speaking, the Camorra could behave this way as they did not fear police retribution. Many police, especially in Coney Island, were on the Camorra's payroll and could be easily plied with a few bribes to look the other way. In addition to this, *omerta* was still a very strong idea at this early stage, and so the Camorra operated under the assumption that *no one*, even on the Morello side, would cooperate with police. Because of these conditions, the Camorra operated with seeming impunity in the period following the 1916 assassinations.

Unfortunately for the Camorra, one of their men would become one of the first key Italian-American criminals to flip and turn witness for law enforcement. The year after Nicolo Morello's assassination, Ralph "The Barber" Daniello a *camorrista* who had been a part of the planning of Nicolo's hit, decided to cooperate with police and is believed to have exposed the activities of the Camorra, their criminal dealings, and the entire plot of Nicolo's murder. His testimony against the Camorra rackets led to a spree of convictions against *camorristas*, as well as a crackdown on police corruption, as Daniello also exposed some of the Camorra's police payroll information.

In 1918, Morano and Vollero were both found guilty in the Nicolo Morello and Charles Ubriaco case, and the pair received twenty years in prison, each. Tony Paretti, another gangster involved in Nicolo's hit and very close associate of Morano, was given a death sentence for his role and was executed in 1927 (it is notable that even after Morano was imprisoned, he refused to cooperate with police, and refused to answer any of the prosecution's questions against Paretti). A year prior to Morano and Vollero's imprisonment, the other Camorra boss, Andrea Ricci, was assassinated. It is likely that his own men carried out the hit, fearing that he too would turn witness.

After Ricci's death, Morano and Vollero's imprisonment, and the litany of charges against other prominent *camorristas*, the Italian-American Camorra was decimated. And so the Mafia-Camorra War ended in a somewhat unusual fashion, with law enforcement doing the bulk of the work and eliminating the Morello Family's targets without the Family having to lift a finger. With the Mafia being the clear victor, the Family expanded their gambling rackets in Manhattan with a major thorn in their side now fully removed. Many of the remaining *camorristas,* most of whom were now out of work and with no real crime structure to return to, ended up joining up with Morello's Mafia. The Family, which had made it through their first major conflict successfully without their leader, and now strengthened by the elimination of the Camorra, was now ready to dominate New York's criminal underworld. The stage was now set for 1920, a seminal year for the Morello Family.

Prohibition and the Castellammarese War

After Nicolo's murder, Giuseppe's other half-brother Vincenzo took control of the Family. Also around the end of the Mafia-Camorra War, Morello captain Joe Masseria was released from prison, where he had been sent in 1913 on a burglary charge. Masseria expanded his power within the Morello Family, and Salvatore D'Aquila, another Morello captain who had broken away after Morello's arrest, began a power struggle with Masseria over dominance in New York City. Masseria was also directly at odds with one of D'Aquila's top men, Umberto Valenti. These struggles would develop into a full-fledged Mafia War in the 1920s.

In 1920, two key events took place for the Morellos. First, in January, the United States government made the sale of alcohol federally illegal. This resulted in a burgeoning new market for the production, sale, and importation of illegal liquor and beer. This presented a lucrative opportunity for the inherently opportunistic Mafia Families, who predictably capitalized on the chance. In very short order, the Mafia ended up having close to a monopoly on bootlegging alcohol, and many prominent Mafia figures came to national prominence—notably, Al Capone and his Chicago organization dubbed "The Outfit."

Also in 1920, founding Mafia Boss Giuseppe Morello was released from prison. Initially intending on returning to a prominent role within the organization, his life was immediately put in danger. Sal D'Aquila, concerned about the competition that Morello might bring and simultaneously fearing his retribution for breaking away from the Family, put out a hit on the newly free Morello. For his own survival, Morello fled back to his homeland of Sicily, where he lived under fear of D'Aquila. While in Sicily, Masseria was Morello's main protector and remained loyal to the highly respected Boss.

Meanwhile, conflict was brewing on the western side of the Atlantic. A series of retribution hits took place between Masseria and the D'Aquila-Valenti alliance from 1920 onwards. Then in 1922, Valenti had ordered a hit on Vincenzo Terranova, current boss of the Morello Family. The hit was successful and several other Morello people were targeted, leaving Joe Masseria as the new official boss of the Family. While Masseria was also targeted in the string of hits, he narrowly survived. Masseria would continue to escape close calls with death and gained a reputation for being untouchable.

Masseria's notoriety continued to grow and as it did, D'Aquila became less and less feared. The continued failed assassination attempts dealt a serious blow to D'Aquila's respectability, and matters would only get worse in August of 1922. Just days after a failed attempt on Masseria's life and after D'Aquila had failed to make progress in the conflict, including failing to eliminate either Giuseppe Morello or Masseria, his ally Valenti was murdered. These events together had ruined D'Aquila's chances of benefitting from the conflict, and the Morellos, led by Joe Masseria, were left as the clear victors. With D'Aquila significantly weakened and the Morellos appearing stronger than ever, the founder of the Family felt confident enough to return to New York City from his Sicilian hiding place. However, Morello apparently had sensed that his time atop the gangster totem pole was over. Understanding that Masseria was now the clear-cut boss of his former Family, Giuseppe Morello became a trusted advisor and *consigliere* to Masseria. Together, the two prospered for years under American prohibition. Salvatore D'Aquila was finally gunned down in 1928, eliminating him as a competitor.

In the mid-1920s, Masseria and Morello continued to expand their racketeering, including their standard loansharking and gambling, but also the incredibly lucrative bootlegged liquor market. In order to bolster the ranks of the Family, Masseria recruited several mafiosi who would end up being prominent figures in the Mafia's history. The most important of these men included Frank Costello, Lucky Luciano, and the future namesake of the Family, Vito Genovese. Each of these men would eventually have their turn at heading the organization. The 1920s was a prosperous period for the Morellos, however with the Mafia-Camorra War still in recent memory, another new conflict was developing.

Sometime after his arrest by the late NYPD Lieutenant Joe Petrosino, mobster Vito Cascio-Ferro had returned to his Sicilian homeland (where he also allegedly had a hand in Petrosino's murder during the latter's Italian investigation). Here, Cascio-Ferro prospered and became a powerful regional boss in Castellammare Del Golfo, a small seaside town in the province of Trapani. Having failed in his earlier attempt to break into the American Mafia scene, he decided to try once more. Sometime in the 1920s, Cascio-Ferro sent one of his top men, Salvatore Maranzano, to attempt to subdue American competition and take control of operations on the other side of the Atlantic. After arriving in the United States, Maranzano soon came to dominate the Castellammarese faction within New York City, which also included prominent gangsters Joe Profaci, Joe Aiello, and a young Giuseppe Bonanno, also known as Joe Bananas.

Maranzano's organization would become involved in two main illicit businesses. The first and most profitable was bootlegging, which included production and sale. Bonanno, at the time, was directly responsible for the protection of the liquor while in transit. The other pot that Maranzano dabbled in was producing forged documents for illegal Italian immigrants. This was an important aspect of the Maranzano business, because many of the smuggled foreigners were Italians who Maranzano would recruit to bolster his ranks. It was the first of these businesses which would put Maranzano at odds with Morello Family boss, Joe Masseria.

Before open hostilities broke out, there were some disputes over stolen liquor beginning around 1928 which exacerbated the tension between the "Americanized" Mafia organization which many of Masseria's men represented, and the newly arrived "old school" Sicilian Castellammarese organization. Around the same time that Masseria was recruiting in preparation for conflict, Maranzano was making similar moves. He attempted to court Charles Luciano; however Luciano was generally put off by the condescending nature of Maranzano and the old school he represented. In particular, Luciano took offense to Maranzano and other Sicilians' aversion to working with non-Italians. Maranzano had made sleights about Luciano's Jewish connections, which clearly was not appreciated. Luciano rejected Maranzano's offers and joined up instead with Masseria, sensing that war was at hand. However, Luciano's loyalties were far from secure, and he too was plotting.

In 1930, the strife developed into a war, generally referred to as the "Castellammarese War." Masseria began violent hostilities by ordering a hit on a Detroit-based Castellammarese by the name of Gaspar Milazzo. Masseria also betrayed an ally of his, Gaetano Reina, whose allies would go on to join Maranzano in order to extract revenge. Maranzano would also launch attacks against Masseria's faction. One of the first Masseria losses was a big one—Giuseppe Morello, a legendary mafioso, founder of the Morello Family, and consigliere to Masseria, was gunned down by Maranzano hitmen in the summer of 1930 at his Harlem office. Months later, Masseria would order a successful hit on another Maranzano ally, this time turning to Chicago-based Joe Aiello. Both of Masseria's early hits, Milazzo and Aiello, were members of the highly influential Italian-American organization, *Unione Siciliana*.

Following the Aiello hit, Maranzano struck back with ruthless intensity. This was possible due to the fact that Maranzano's crew was already far more organized than Masseria, despite the fact that many Castellammarese were relatively new arrivals to the country and to the American Mafia landscape. Maranzano's established connections in Sicily certainly aided this, as well as the Castellammare connection which provided Maranzano with support in other cities such as Chicago, Detroit, and Philadelphia. Several hits on important Masseria men were carried out, followed by several defections from Masseria's crew over to Maranzano. The defections were unsurprising, as many of Masseria's men allegedly expressed doubt, even before the war began, over whether the old timer Masseria was the right man to lead the Family into the 1930s. After much of Masseria's leadership structure was disrupted, he was left with very little options to strike back and began to appear weaker and weaker. Still not having conceded, some of Masseria's men sought a way of ending the destructive conflict. Luciano, plotting from the beginning, saw an opportunity with the help of Vito Genovese.

Luciano and Genovese had reached out to and got in contact with Maranzano to see what kind of deal could be reached. Luciano was clearly after a leadership position, and was willing to betray Masseria to gain control over his organization. However, he understood that there would not be much of a crew to take over if the war continued much longer. So, Luciano agreed to organize a hit on Masseria. In return, Maranzano agreed to officially end the war and bloodshed, and to put Luciano in charge of Masseria's crew which would be subservient to

Maranzano. Before Luciano could make his move, Masseria allegedly discovered the plot and ordered a hit on Luciano while feigning ignorance of his plot. Another of Masseria's men, Joey Adonis, warned Luciano of the plot, and he was able to take action faster than Masseria. Unaware that Adonis, the man he entrusted with Luciano's hit, had flipped on him and allied with Luciano himself, Masseria agreed to a meeting at a restaurant on Coney Island in 1931. At this meeting, Masseria was shot dead during a game of cards by some of his most trusted allies. Genovese was among them.

With Masseria eliminated and Luciano having fulfilled his side of the bargain, Maranzano officially ended the Castellammarese War and brought an end to the bloodshed, at least for a time. Maranzano gave Luciano his blessing to take over the former Morello Family, which soon after became known officially as the Luciano Family. Acknowledging the power of Maranzano, who would soon after declare himself the new Boss of Bosses, Luciano would serve as one of his high ranking lieutenants. Luciano did not forget his friends: Vito Genovese, Frank Costello, Joey Adonis, as well as Luciano's close Jewish associate Bugsy Siegel, all benefited from the rise of Lucky Luciano, who was now at the highest position he had ever achieved. However, his scheming was not quite finished.

Chapter 3:

The Luciano Era

For much of the 1930s, the Genovese Family was centered around Charles "Lucky" Luciano, one of the most well-known mobsters in American history. Representing a new age for the Italian–American Mafia, Luciano's time as Boss was marked by several innovations and lasting achievements. His short reign was a turning point for organized crime.

The Five Families

With Masseria gone and with an array of competent gangsters working under him, Salvatore Maranzano had established himself as the most powerful Mafia figure in New York City. He seemed untouchable. However, the competent men under him were also highly ambitious, and Maranzano's tenure atop the gangster totem pole would prove short-lived. His old-style ways and tendency to absorb his subordinates' rackets would end up upsetting all the wrong people, many of whom had departed from Masseria's gang for all the same reasons. Once again, trouble was brewing in the Mafia underworld.

One of Maranzano's first moves after ending the Castellammarese War was to reorganize the New York Mafia into the now infamous "Five Families" (used as the inspiration for *The Godfather*'s Five Families: The fictional Barzini, Tattaglia, Cuneo, Stracci, and Corleone Families). This move was meant to give the New York City organizations a more strict structure and to make the controlling and administration of the various Families more efficient. The reorganization also led to a solidification of the Mafia hierarchy. No longer were there vague acquaintances with undefined statuses and loose command structures. Now, Each Family was to be organized under the "Boss > Underboss > *Caporegimes* >

Soldiers > Associates" format, with non-Italians being excluded from official membership (an earlier annoyance to Luciano). The Families at the time were headed by Joe Profaci, Tommy Gagliano, Vincent Mangano, and of course Lucky Luciano and Maranzano himself. There was also an unofficial "Sixth Family" that came into prominence in the 1970s—The Rizzutos, led by Nicolo Rizzuto and based in Montreal, Quebec, Canada. The Rizzutos had close ties with New York Families, and had become famous for their initial alliance with the Bonanno Family and their eventual betrayal with the 1981 Rizzuto-orchestrated assassinations of three Bonanno *caporegimes*.

Soon after the end of the War and the "Five Families" reorganization, Maranzano organized a banquet in New York and a large celebration in his own honor. Various prominent American mafiosi were in attendance. Maranzano took this opportunity to announce himself as the new *capo di tutti capi*—Boss of Bosses. To many of Maranzano's underlings, this move signaled what they had feared: Life under Maranzano would be much the same as under Joe Masseria. The declaration was a particular annoyance to Luciano, who did not like the concept of a singular "Boss of Bosses" who controlled the entire underworld. Luciano now came to see Maranzano as potentially even worse than Masseria—he was greedy and willing to scheme to acquire more power. Needless to say, in an organization where everyone is out to get rich, excessive greed is never a popular character trait.

Only months after being named Maranzano's lieutenant, Luciano had decided to make a move against the new *capo di tutti capi*. Around the same time however, Maranzano grew paranoid, and correctly feared that Luciano and his growing power base were becoming a serious threat. Especially worrying was Luciano's ascent within the leadership structure of the *Unione Siciliana*. Maranzano needed to act fast and tried to get the jump on Luciano before he was killed himself, but once again, the loyalty of Luciano's friends saved his life. Fellow mobster and future head of the modern Lucchese Family, Tommy Lucchese, heard whispers of the hit and delivered the news to Luciano. As it turned out, Maranzano wanted Luciano, Costello, and Genovese, the three most important men in the Family, all dead.

On September 10, 1931, armed men disguised as law enforcement set out to kill Salvatore Maranzano, the Boss of Bosses. The man in charge of the hit was apparently Abraham "Bo" Weinberg, a Jewish gangster and bootlegger based in Manhattan and closely associated with bootlegging legend Dutch Schultz. Lucchese himself allegedly also went along in order to identify Maranzano for the hitmen, all of whom were unfamiliar to the boss. At the time, Maranzano was in his expensive office in the New York Central Building, also known as the Helmsley building, a newly-erected palatial skyscraper on Park Avenue in Manhattan. This office functioned as his headquarters for his migrant smuggling and document forgery rackets. It was here that Maranzano had ordered Luciano, Costello, and Genovese to a meeting—one which Luciano believed would have been their last.

Just a short while before Luciano's would-be murderer had arrived at Maranzano's office to await the three targets, Bo Weinberg and his disguised co-assassins entered his office and ordered the men inside to surrender. Because Maranzano and his associates generally avoided working with non-Italians, his men did not recognize the Jewish gangsters posing as federal agents. It was Luciano's Jewish connection, which Maranzano found repellant, that had allowed Lucky to get the drop on him. The men had stripped Maranzano's bodyguards of their weapons, leaving him defenseless. Maranzano, who had been *capo di tutti capi* for only about five months, was found dead in his office with numerous gunshot and stab wounds. He was the only casualty.

Maranzano was not the only victim that day—Luciano and his Family had orchestrated a massive, relatively simultaneous series of hits on Maranzano allies. Estimates range between 30 and 90 total Maranzano associates killed all across the country. It was carried out over the following few days, but many of the hits occurred within the hour of Maranzano's shooting. The most conservative sources claim that no such planned "mass assassination" even took place. Regardless, Maranzano's Family and his nation-wide connections had been eliminated, and the Sicilian Mafia "old guard" had been absolutely decimated. The struggle between those who represented old style traditionalism and those who embraced Americanization, which came to a head during the Castellammarese War, was now over, and it was Luciano's youthful and more open-minded peers who were left victorious.

It has been alleged that Vincent Coll, a noted Mafia hitman and the one hired for $25,000 USD to assassinate Luciano, Costello, and Genovese, was approaching the entrance to Maranzano's office building just as the hit squad was fleeing. Coll himself then quickly fled. This was not the first time Coll had become entangled with Weinberg and the rest of Schultz' crew. Earlier that year, in summer 1931, Coll had been directed to murder Schultz associate Joseph Rao, who worked with Schultz in bootlegging. Coll became infamous after his attempted hit, not because it was a high profile killing, but because it was a massive failure which did not result in Rao's death, but instead the shooting of several children, including one who died—the tragedy earned Coll the nickname "Mad Dog." It was not until after the failed assassination on Park Avenue in September that Coll was tried and eventually acquitted. However, his time was soon up. In 1932, Schultz eliminated Coll and much of his crew. Weinberg, the main component of the Maranzano hit, was also involved in Coll's murder.

After Maranzano's death and the destruction of his ally network, Charles "Lucky" Luciano became the most powerful Mafia boss in New York, with strong underlings in Vito Genovese and Frank Costello. It would have been entirely unsurprising if Luciano took the opportunity to declare himself the new *capo di tutti capi*, as would have been the expected custom at the time. But Luciano, who had had an issue with the unofficial title since at least the Masseria era, refused to do so. Instead, he "abolished" the title, deeming it a source of unnecessary competition, resentment, and friction between the Families. In any case, Luciano was generally averse to media attention, and likely would not have wanted to be placed in such a prominent position anyway. In the years leading up to his final ascent within the underworld, media references to Luciano were extremely rare—he was a man who preferred to keep a low profile. It has also been suggested that Luciano, a revolutionary in many ways, was also keen on abolishing the ceremony used to induct "Made Men" into Mafia Families. In his crusade against the Sicilian Mafia's old style ways, he had come to believe that the ceremonial and symbolic traditions of the Mafia were unnecessary. Interestingly, it was Vito Genovese who allegedly convinced Luciano to not abandon the concept of "Made Men."

With Luciano's dominance now unchallenged, he wasted no time in expanding his criminal enterprise, as well as that of other Mafia Families. The Luciano Family operated in the usual markets: Loansharking, extortion, and gambling. However, Luciano also spread out into other markets. He greatly expanded his prostitution ring, became deeply involved in union racketeering and drug trafficking, and was instrumental in the Mafia's takeover of Manhattan's Waterfront and Garment District businesses. However, with the position of Boss of Bosses now gone and no clear head of all Mafia activities, Luciano needed a way to maintain control of the organization he had fought and schemed to dominate. To that end, he called a meeting in late 1931 in Chicago, which most mafiosi likely assumed would be his ceremony to announce himself *capo di tutti capi*. At this meeting of several powerful Mafia bosses, Luciano proposed something that to this day is generally regarded as his crowning achievement and greatest contribution to the Mafia world—The Commission.

The Commission

From the beginning of Luciano's reign, he had been trying to conceive of a way to revolutionize both the structure and methodology of the Mafia. Luciano was disdainful of what he considered to be pointless conflicts between Families: Turf wars, retribution killings, and the like. In order for everyone to succeed, petty squabbles needed to be kept at a minimum. After all, years' worth of infighting had left Sicilian-American organized crime more vulnerable to the government and its law enforcement agencies. The more mafiosi who get arrested and prosecuted, the likelier it will be that their operations are exposed. Every Mafia Family in the country did indeed have a common enemy.

What Luciano proposed was a national, confederation-style governmental body for the Mafia; a body which would meet at regular intervals to discuss the most pressing issues that the Mafia faced as a whole. Its mandate would be to serve as a mediator or arbiter in disputes involving two or more mafiosi or Families, with the ideal outcome being to avoid an escalation of violence. Disputes of all kinds could be taken to this body, which would also serve as an overseer of

Mafia activities. For example, it would be incumbent upon mobsters seeking to take reasonably drastic action (as we will see, this includes political assassination) to first make a case to this governing body and seek its approval.

In this way, The Commission would serve both to reduce the amount of infighting within the organizations as well as reduce the public spectacle of the Mafia by reining in "loose cannons" or independent actors. It was also at this meeting that the lasting tradition of Made Men being "untouchable" originated. It was decided that Made Men would be immune from hits by non-Made gangsters. Only another Made Man could authorize and carry out a hit like that, whereas the killing of a Made Man by an outsider would be punishable by retribution murder. In Al Capone's home turf of Chicago, the body which would come to be known as "The Commission" was approved by a panel of national Mafia figures and peers of Luciano.

The fact that The Commission exists is another testament to the Mafia's aforementioned "popular associationism," referring to the tendency to insert itself into legitimate institutions. This can be seen at both at the micro level, with Families using honest businesses as fronts or as laundering hubs, and at the macro level, with Families becoming involved in both regional and national politics. Now, we can see the Mafia constructing a new kind of institution based on established American political and commercial ones. The name "The Commission" evokes images of political congressional committees, and the body even had a "board of directors" which served as its highest administrative panel, clearly based on corporate leadership boards and investment groups. The Commission, which has been likened to a kind of Mafia Supreme Court, represented the new age of the fully Americanized Sicilian Mafia. Much in the spirit of American values, the American Mafia had divorced itself wholly from their old world ancestors.

The Commission's first set of directors for the board were seven prominent mob figures. This included the boss of each of New York City's Five Families. Vincent Mangano, Joe Profaci, Tommy Gagliano, and Luciano were familiar faces, but Joseph Bonanno, a former underling of Maranzano and a survivor of the Castellammarese War, was the new boss of the freshly renamed Family. Also included in the board of directors was Stefano Magaddino, also known as "The Undertaker," a powerful Mafia boss based in Buffalo, NY. His influence stretched as far north as Montreal, QC, a city which the Sicilian-Canadian Rizzuto Family would come to dominate in the 1970s. The seventh spot on the board was occupied by perhaps the most famous mafioso and bootlegger of all time: Chicago-based and American-born Alphonse "Scarface" Capone, whose domination of crime in the Midwest United States couldn't be ignored. Lucky Luciano served as the first chairman of the board of directors.

Aside from serving as a peacekeeping body, The Commission also enabled a greater level of cooperation between Mafia organizations in distant parts of the country. Alliance networks became national rather than regional, and it became possible to co-operate on large, interstate business ventures. Further, it helped eliminate a great amount of animosity which had been bred into the Mafia. Luciano had earned himself a tremendous amount of goodwill in the national underworld, since he was unquestionably the most powerful boss in the country yet refused to take the title. Although he served as chairman, it was Luciano who insisted that The Commission be run along democratic lines, and that each member Family have a vote in decisions, with each vote carrying equal weight as all the others. And, in an attempt to dissuade power hungry opportunists, The Commission would also be responsible for approving new Family bosses.

To many, Luciano epitomized the concept of the selfless boss, one who was most concerned with cooperative prosperity rather than greed, revenge, and megalomania. Speaking on the subject, Luciano has been recorded explaining his motives: "I explained to 'em we was in a business that hadda keep movin' without explosions every two minutes, knockin' guys off just because they come from a different part of Sicily, that kinda crap was giving us a bad name, and we couldn't cooperate until it stopped" (Gosch and Hammer, 2013). By Mafia boss standards, Lucky Luciano was certainly unique.

To a large degree, Luciano's Mafia Revolution was a success. The meetings meant to establish The Commission went unnoticed by law enforcement, and thus the largest Mafia administrative structure ever built was set up right under their noses. Families enjoyed more security and profitability than during the prior war-torn era of the Mafia-

Camorra and Castellammarese conflicts. Nineteen thirty-one in the United States was a period of unprecedented economic insecurity, unemployment, and crippling poverty. The financial position of most Americans was completely undermined, but the Mafia dealt with no such hardships. Under Luciano's new organizational structure, the Mafia's monopoly on vice prospered while others floundered through the early years of the Great Depression.

The new system was also designed to curb the high turnover rate of Family bosses. Bringing more peace and cooperation reduced the risk of bosses being murdered by rivals, but the new system also helped to remove bosses further from the actual illicit activities being committed by lower ranking members. In this way, Bosses would also be further protected from criminal prosecutors. This too was a success, and the lower rates of turnover for heads of Families helped foster more stability and longer lasting alliances across the board. Somewhat unfairly, Luciano turned out to be the only high ranking Mafia member in his era to receive any kind of major sentencing. Unfortunately for him, his convictions would come a mere few years after he had revolutionized organized crime.

For the first few years after its inception, The Commission did not face any major trials as operations ran smoothly. This would change in 1935 after prosecutor Thomas Dewey began investigating the Mafia. Dewey was a crusader in many ways, and aggressively pursued Mafia operations. For this reason, he was appointed Special Prosecutor by New York's governor at the time, Herbert Lehman, in response to accusations of soft-handedness toward Mafia activities in New York City. It was believed that the state government was focusing too much energy on combating the alleged Communist threat, while letting organized crime run rampant through New York.

With the assistance of noted NYC Mayor Fiorello "the little flower" La Guardia, Dewey began recruiting for his campaign against the mob. La Guardia also was an aggressive advocate of eliminating Mafia crime. Vito Genovese largely escaped the 1930s persecution: It instead was Luciano and Costello who felt his wrath. In a devastating move for Mafia heads, Dewey also lobbied to amend New York's existing legislation that disallowed multiple charges and defendants to be heard under a single trial. This law meant that prosecuting top Mafia figures, who would only be tangentially connected to the actual crimes, was incredibly difficult. After Dewey successfully changed the legislation, handling multiple charges under one trial allowed for multiple connections to be made leading up to the boss of the Family. Invigorated, Dewey's team then aggressively pursued a number of criminal enterprises which the Mafia was known for, including the Mafia-run Italian lottery as well as prostitution. It was the latter that would ultimately cause Luciano's initial downfall.

One of the earliest successes of Dewey's investigation was the case his team had built on Jewish gangster and Luciano associate Dutch Schultz. Schultz had been known to Dewey for some time and had been indicted in 1933, and after the first trial against Schultz ended without substantial progress, the prosecution threatened him with a conviction for tax evasion. Schultz grew more paranoid and erratic as the proceedings went along. Eventually, Schultz resolved to murder Dewey in order to disrupt the investigation against him and remove the top law enforcement predator at the time. This would have been a radical move, even for the Mafia. Under previous circumstances, Schultz could have acted of his own volition and carried out the hit with his own men. However, this was the era of Luciano and The Commission.

Abiding by the new system, Schultz called a meeting with The Commission in 1935 and sought permission to carry out the hit, arguing that Dewey's presence was a threat to the entire Mafia, not just himself. He wasn't wrong. However, The Commission and its board of directors correctly viewed this as a step too far. Though it was true that eliminating Dewey would delay all Mafia investigations and remove a powerful anti-mob crusader from the picture, it was also true that the assassination of such a prominent national figure who was in the middle of a massive investigation into the Mafia would undoubtedly bring a firestorm of attention to the Mafia and would likely result in an even more brutal national crackdown. Schultz, a respected and well-connected gangster, had his request for permission denied.

Unfortunately for Schultz, this only enraged him and made him even more desperate. He disregarded The Commission's decision and told the chairmen that he would kill Dewey anyway, before storming off. Sometime after, fellow mobster Albert Anastasia came to Luciano with news that Schultz had set the wheels in motion for eliminating Dewey. Obviously, Schultz' erratic behavior and disobedience toward the new high authority could not be tolerated. After deliberating, The Commission had resolved to murder Schultz before he could do irreparable damage to the organization.

In October of 1935, Schultz was shot by a hit squad while meeting with associates at the Newark restaurant-pub Palace Chop House. A hit squad associated with Anastasia entered the restaurant and fired shots into Schultz and all three of his associates. None died instantly, and the assassins were driven off before all four were taken away in ambulances. The situation deteriorated at the hospital, and all of the men eventually died the next day. Interestingly, Schultz had allegedly converted to Catholicism while attempting to sway Luciano's decision on his assassination plot, and apparently had requested baptism at the hospital before he died. In the end, it was Schultz' fiery temper, which likely led to most of his success, that resulted in his death. Schultz was now gone and a potential crisis averted, but the threat posed by Dewey was still looming.

Luck Runs Out

After Dutch Schultz had been eliminated as a candidate for prosecution, Dewey steered his crusade toward the *de facto* head of the American Mafia: Lucky Luciano himself. As a result of Luciano's character and business ethic, he was a relatively unknown figure, despite being the most powerful gangster in the country. Even to many law enforcement agents, he was a non-entity. Dewey however, though likely not knowing the extent of Luciano's power, certainly knew he was a high ranking mob-affiliated criminal, given his unsavory connections and the disparity between his recorded income and obviously high living standards. Income fraud and tax evasion were at the time one of the few reliable methods to convict Mafia bosses, and so Luciano's finances were scrutinized carefully by Dewey and his team. Luciano was now firmly in the crosshairs of the Dewey crusade.

Another key figure in Luciano's downfall was an assistant District Attorney named Eunice Carter. Carter became chiefly concerned with investigating the prostitution rings operated by the Mafia, one of Luciano's biggest rackets, and encouraged Dewey to look closer at prostitution rather than tax or income crimes. Carter organized and led raids in dozens of suspected brothels in New York City. The tactics Carter used proved ingenious and highly effective. In a time where the Mafia was organized more than ever and *omerta* was still taken very seriously, it was difficult for law enforcement to gather willing and cooperative witnesses from within Mafia structures. Even Jewish gangsters such as Schultz' companions during his 1935 assassination refused to give any information about their attackers to the police while in the hospital, until explicitly given permission to by their superior.

Given this state of affairs, Carter and Dewey instead pursued those with intimate knowledge of the operations but who were not bound by any code of silence: The prostitutes themselves. During the raids, numerous prostitutes and women who ran the brothels were arrested and threatened with being charged for soliciting prostitution. Dewey's team quickly realized that the prostitutes, many of whom claimed to have been habitually abused by Mafia members and associates, were more than willing to cooperate with law enforcement in exchange for protection and an escape from harsh prison time. It is possible, however, that the information provided by the prostitutes was embellished; not giving the investigators the information they wanted to hear could have meant their imprisonment.

Over the course of the interviews with prostitutes and madams, Luciano had been, for the first time, directly implicated in a crime. He was outed as the leader of a massive prostitution crime ring in the United States, referred to simply as "The Combination." The ring consisted of hundreds of locations and thousands of prostitutes in Brooklyn and Manhattan alone. It was also discovered by Dewey's team that Davie Betillo, a known Luciano associate, had been running the administration of a huge number of organized brothels in the area. Information obtained through careful wiretapping of Luciano's brothels only strengthened the case against him.

After the raids, Luciano realized that Dutch Schultz' fears about Dewey were completely justified. He feared that he would soon be exposed, and briefly fled New York City for Arkansas. The city of Hot Springs had a notoriously corrupt local government, one that was easily plied by powerful and well-connected mafiosi. The city had become something of a haven for gangsters on the lam. The investigation proceeded in his absence, and eventually Dewey's team sought to nail Luciano on nearly one hundred counts of organizing forced prostitution in NYC. Cooperating with the investigation, the state of Arkansas intended on shipping Luciano back to New York, and had him arrested pending his hearing. However, a man like Luciano was unlikely to flee to a place where he did not have friends in high places. His bail was posted by Hot Springs' very own chief detective.

Luciano was once again free, but it would not last. Dewey knew Luciano's whereabouts (apparently, a detective friend of Dewey's had recognized Lucky's face and quickly tipped off the lead investigator), and bribing Arkansas state officials yielded no results. Before Luciano's Family and legal team could act to protect him, the investigators stormed his Arkansas safe haven and took him by force. Dewey's team extracted him back to New York City with a heavy security detail, fearing that the Luciano Family would attempt a rescue. He was set to face trial on prostitution charges, along with several of his Mafia associates.

In May of 1936, Luciano's trial began. Dewey served as the lead prosecutor and assembled a massive lineup of dozens of prostitutes, madams, and pimps to serve as witnesses against Lucky. The witnesses reliably testified that they had been taken advantage of by the operators of The Combination. The hardships brought on by the Great Depression forced them into a desperate search for income, and Dewey made sure to emphasize that the men on trial took advantage of people at their lowest points. Dewey's entire strategy revolved around framing Luciano as a savage, immoral pimp, while also building him up as the most important orchestrator and architect of The Combination.

The actual degree of Luciano's involvement in The Combination is debated, however it mattered little at the time. Under Dewey's guidance, multiple members of his witness lineup testified that Luciano was the man at the top of the chain of command within the prostitution ring. It did not help Luciano's case that many of the prostitute witnesses also testified to the brutal abuse they suffered as disciplinary action carried out by men directly under Luciano's command. Prostitutes who misbehaved or did not earn enough were apparently routinely threatened, beaten, and sometimes physically disfigured. Dewey had clearly won the moral argument in the case.

The main arguments used in defense of Luciano mostly fell flat. His team attempted to paint Dewey as an opportunistic careerist, who was leading this crusade simply to glorify his own name and boost his career. They also were sure to point out the fact that the most damning testimonies made against Luciano were from witnesses who were admitted drug addicts and criminals who could not be trusted. Meanwhile, Luciano played dumb. He claimed to have never met any of the supposed "witnesses," and even claimed to be unacquainted with his co-defendants who were present at the same trial (this had been the first joint trial under New York's new regulations). Ever charismatic, Luciano even joked that although he certainly gave money to brothels, he never profited from them.

These efforts were in vain. Despite his defense's insistence that Dewey was unprofessional and only seeking a reputation, the lead prosecutor expertly dismantled Luciano's story. Quick to point out inconsistencies in his testimony, Dewey had had Luciano on the ropes for the majority of the trial, and it showed—Luciano was allegedly visibly distraught as Dewey proceeded with his examination. Dewey also exposed Luciano's obvious tax fraud. Luciano led an aristocratic life, and despite his general avoidance of attention, his lavish lifestyle was well known. Dewey drew the jury's attention to a massive discrepancy: According to the United States government, Luciano officially lived on a yearly income of less than $25,000 USD. Luciano's quick wittedness failed him, and he was unable to explain himself. His well-known ties to the infamous Al Capone did not help either.

In a serious reputational blow, Dewey and the prosecution were also able to get Luciano to admit that he, at one time in his mid-1920s, had broken the *omerta* code of silence. He had apparently co-operated with police in order to aid an investigation into a drug distributor. Although, the respect that Luciano commanded remained largely intact, even after the boss went to prison. Despite the fact that Dewey's case against Luciano was not by any means damning on a technical level, Lucky had talked himself into a corner. It turned out to be a massive mistake to allow Luciano to take the witness stand, and it was very likely Luciano's own nerves and discomposure that doomed him. In June of 1936, his jury voted to convict on the prostitution charges, and Charles "Lucky" Luciano was sentenced to 30 to 50 years in prison.

Luciano was now put away for decades and Dewey had been launched into the national spotlight. Exactly as Luciano's legal team suggested, Dewey received a huge reputational and professional windfall from the guilty verdict. He went on to become the Governor of New York and even led a successful campaign for the Republican presidential nomination during World War II (unsurprisingly, however, Democrat Franklin D. Roosevelt would win, claiming his fourth consecutive presidential victory). He even served as the basis for a lead character in the 1937 film *Marked Woman*, played by acting legend Humphrey Bogart. The man was now famous, and it all stemmed from a trial that is highly debated to this day. Luciano was certainly a criminal and deserved a stint in prison, however the facts of the case for which he was tried are nonetheless disputed. Luciano's was not the only story that did not add up, and many of Dewey's witnesses were certainly testifying out of fear of being imprisoned themselves. Whether or not this was done under duress from Mafia thugs, it is noteworthy that most of the key witnesses in the trial ended up retracting their testimonies sometime after the conviction.

Luciano had been sent to New York's Clinton Penitentiary in the town of Dannemora, a maximum-security facility. His life was by no means harsh, and it's been reported that Luciano's life was as close to kingly as was possible in prison. It is likely that many prison guards and officials feared retribution if he was treated harshly; his criminal credentials were nationally known by this point. Luciano was meant to remain here for up to 50 years, which very well could have meant that he would die in prison. But that was not Luciano's fate.

He would continue his fascinating life during the Second World War. In 1942, Luciano and the United States Navy had meetings, facilitated in part by Luciano associate Meyer Lansky. At the time, the military was concerned about possible Axis infiltration in the country through the New York waterfront, a major point of entry for European immigrants. They also knew that the organization, of which Luciano was still the leader, dominated this area. In return for intelligence, the government offered to release Luciano from prison. After the end of the war, Luciano was indeed released, but on the condition that he be deported to and remain within Italy. Luciano was released in 1946, and from prison went to Sicily, to Cuba, and back to Sicily, continuing his mafioso life all the while. He finally died in Napoli of a heart attack in 1962.

Luciano remained the official Boss of the Luciano Family for his entire time in prison. But, despite his relative freedom and comfort within the prison walls, he was obviously unable to run the day-to-day operations of the organization. So, Luciano allegedly looked to his underboss, Vito Genovese. Genovese was a long-time ally of Luciano and had been by his side through the Castellammarese War and the seizing of control from Sal Maranzano. Genovese, technically only an acting boss serving in Luciano's place, was now in control of the organization which would soon bear his name. But his power was almost immediately put under threat.

Chapter 4:

Don Vito

The man for whom the Genovese Family is named had led a fascinating and turbulent life, especially after his initial appointment as Lucky Luciano's acting boss. From his beginnings in the area around Napoli to being a petty thug in Little Italy, Vito steadily climbed the Mafia ladder, being a reliable man through prohibition and several Mafia wars. Genovese was eventually put in charge in Luciano's absence, was forced to abdicate, worked both sides of World War II, and eventually made a triumphant return as kingpin of the New York underworld. This chapter will detail the life of one of the most consequential gangsters in New York criminal history, and Anthony DeStefano's recent authoritative book *The Deadly Don* (2021) offers us fresh insight into the life of the boss from Napoli.

The Neapolitan Don

Vito Genovese was born in 1897 in a subdivision of the town of Tufino, named Ricigliano. Born just 30 kilometers away from Napoli, Genovese was the first non-Sicilian Boss of the Family that Giuseppe Morello had formed decades prior. Also unlike many older mafiosi, including Morello, Genovese did not leave the old country due to criminal prosecutions resulting from prior Mafia activity. Vito left Italy when he was only 15 or 16, having no known history of involvement in organized crime. Arriving aboard the *SS Taormina* in 1913, Vito and his family settled in the Italian neighborhood in Manhattan, where his father had immigrated to eight years earlier. It is possible that the family had fled because of the recent increased activity of Mount Vesuvius, the famous volcano that wiped out Pompeii. Many in nearby Napoli feared an eruption. What is more likely, however, is that Vito's mother sensed that a major European conflict was on the horizon and feared for the safety of her children. She was vindicated, of course: World War I would erupt just 14 months after teenage Vito arrived in New York City.

As a youth in Little Italy, it would only take the future boss a few years to turn to a life of crime. He mostly engaged in petty theft and robbery, but also came to be known by several mafiosi by serving as an errand boy. The latter was a fairly common practice in Mafia-controlled areas. One of his key responsibilities was running the numbers routes, which involved going around the neighborhood and collecting bet money for the Mafia's Italian lottery. Then in 1917 when Vito was only 19 years old, he was arrested for the first time. The charge was possessing an illegal firearm, and the young Genovese pled guilty. The teen was sentenced, but the circumstances and climate of World War I potentially offered Vito an opportunity. The United States government attempted to draft him.

Believing that service in the United States military would offer Vito an easier path to citizenship, Genovese was initially eager to join up. Vito had been shipped off to a military base in New York for assessment, apparently fully intending to fight overseas. Perhaps fortunately for Vito, however, the First World War was nearing its end. By the time the final ceasefire took effect near the end of 1918, Vito had not yet been deployed, and the war officially ended before Vito ever served a day overseas. The Second World War would be a far more eventful few years for the adult Genovese.

Over the next few years, Vito had very little trouble with the law. Aside from another arrest on a murder charge about a year after his initial jailing, which turned out to be a false alarm, Vito managed to stay off the radar of New York City law enforcement for years until he was 26 years old. At this point, Genovese had become involved in the lucrative bootlegging business, and he was undoubtedly in association with Mafia men. In May of 1924, a vehicle that Genovese was a passenger in was involved in a violent single car collision. In an era where vehicle safety standards were minimal, 26 year old Vito was launched out of the car when it drove straight into a tree at high speed. Vito was seriously injured, but survived. Unfortunately, multiple weapons were found by the car when emergency services arrived.

According to New York police, Genovese and his three associates had been fleeing from someone, almost certainly a rival bootlegger and his goons. The police tied the incident to an earlier bootlegging related shooting in Manhattan, and believed that a similar confrontation had just occurred on Coney Island, from which Vito and his companions were forced to flee. At the scene of the crash, police had found Vito injured, another passenger dead (he had collided directly with the tree that the car had struck), and the driver missing.

Police threatened Genovese with a vehicular homicide charge, most likely in order to scare a confession out of him. Realizing that there was no way it would hold up in court (because, of course, Genovese had not been driving that night), neither Genovese nor his associates said a word about what had happened. Genovese's gamble paid off, and he had charges dropped yet again. His story never changed. According to Genovese himself, he and his companions were simply gone for dinner and a night out on Coney Island. Driving home in the rain, "all of a sudden" the car veered off and smashed into a tree (DeStefano, 2021). Though the police obviously didn't believe this, there was no concrete evidence that Vito had committed any crimes, despite the weapons discovered by police. In fact, Genovese would get lucky on a number of gun charges throughout his life, and was even charged with murder in 1925. He always seemed to slip through the hands of the NYPD.

By the time this took place, Genovese was almost certainly already working under "Joe the Boss" Masseria. Genovese was involved in bootlegging along with other, mostly Italian, gangsters. Joe Masseria was the Italian bootlegging kingpin, especially after D'Aquila's 1928 assassination. After all, bootlegging was the most profitable illicit industry at the time (an estimated 30,000 illegal pub establishments were in operation in New York City alone during prohibition). Along with Al Capone, Frank Costello, Gaetano Reina, and Lucky Luciano, Vito Genovese learned the ins and outs of Mafia life under the tutelage of Masseria, who clearly had inducted some of the most famous gangsters in history into the Mafia. Still an underling, Vito had no idea that he was now a part of the organization which he would rule and lend his name to in the coming decades.

While working under Masseria, the Luciano-Costello-Genovese trio also began working with Jewish gangsters. Meyer Lansky was among them, one of Luciano's most reliable associates throughout his reign. Arnold Rothstein, another Jewish gangster, was also instrumental. Known for his intellect, Rothstein was fundamental in guiding Luciano and his cohorts on the logistics of bootlegging liquor as a racket. The three men would soon begin their own bootlegging operation, which was funded largely by Rothstein. This was a common theme in the Mafia: Jewish gangsters, prized for their intellectual prowess and financial savvy, were often used to fund projects and plan the efficient operation of the rackets. Within the trio, however, it was Costello who was seen as the brains of the operation. Costello organized the shipping and storage of illegal liquor at the so-called "Rum Row," the eastern seaboard where liquor shipments were smuggled into the United States. Costello also oversaw the key condition of smuggling: Paying off police officers and city officials to look the other way.

Costello would become a relatively well-known figure during prohibition (interestingly, although *The Godfather* character of Vito Corleone was inspired by an amalgamation of different gangsters, it was Costello who provided the wise, elder statesman style character that Corleone's character would embody). In his work with Jewish (and Irish) gangsters, Costello became an exceedingly wealthy man, which he used to empower his own position. In the grand scheme of things, Costello is certainly overshadowed by Luciano and Genovese, but his work during this time cannot be underestimated. Costello had establishments set up all over New York City to both warehouse and distribute the liquor that he had smuggled in through the harbor. Needless to say, he was a target. Genovese, however, maintained a relatively low profile during prohibition, possibly as a result of his shocking number of close calls with law enforcement during his earlier years. This paid off: Costello and his higher up associates faced numerous charges against them for bootlegging, not Genovese. In some cases, this left the bootleggers, some of whom had amassed tens of millions of dollars in fortune, flat out bankrupt.

Meanwhile, Genovese was still profiting handsomely from his operations, but drew considerably less legal attention. He had also begun dabbling in the counterfeiting business, one of the oldest Mafia activities in the United States, dating back to Giuseppe Morello's cross-Atlantic counterfeit currency ring. Genovese operated mostly in gold certificates, a form of legal currency in the United States up until the mid-1930s. This proved very profitable as well for Vito, and the extremely high quality of the notes that his operation produced had shook the U.S. government all the way up to Washington, D.C.

Genovese's absence from media headlines and the minds of law enforcement would soon come to an end, however. In May of 1930, one of the counterfeiting hubs that Genovese had a hand in operating was raided by federal agents. The agents found enough material in the building to produce over $4 million in counterfeit U.S. dollars. Genovese was not present at the counterfeiting hub at the time of the raid, but this was not *exactly* a stroke of good luck. Genovese was still implicated in the crime of operating the printing press which produced the counterfeit notes, and he ended up being named in several of the charges brought against the forgers. The three Genovese associates that were found within the building during the raid all delivered guilty pleas. Genovese, however, was a tougher customer. Not because of his water-tight alibi or shrewd legal team or reliable witnesses to the defense. It was because the prosecution quite literally could not find him. After several thorough manhunts for Vito, the prosecution eventually gave up, and the court dismissed his racketeering, counterfeiting, and conspiracy charges.

Although Vito avoided conviction yet again, he could no longer maintain his lowkey reputation. After over a decade of criminal activity, Vito finally received the media attention he probably already deserved years prior. The newspaper headlines identified him as a powerful and dangerous Mafia leader. He would soon make an even bigger name for himself, as Joe Masseria's time as *capo di tutti capi* was nearing its end. Gaetano Reina, another of the younger mafiosi associated with Genovese et al. and working under Masseria, was shot dead in early 1930 under the orders of Masseria. This was apparently done in retribution for Reina refusing to surrender even more of his profits from his rackets to Masseria, a request which many of the boss' underlings already found aggressive. It was this move which, in part, spurred Genovese, Luciano, Costello, and Bonanno to move against Masseria. After witnessing the obvious change of tide in the rivalry between Masseria and Maranzano, this group of Americanized mafiosi turned their allegiance over to the Castellammarese boss.

The story of Luciano and company under Maranzano has already been detailed. While it has been established that Luciano viewed Maranzano as even more of a problem than Masseria, it is debated what the prime motivating factor was in Luciano's decision to move against the new top boss. Some claim it was the Jewish sect of gangsters, who were close allies of Luciano, who convinced Lucky that the only option was to eliminate Maranzano. It is also possible that Luciano was seriously irked by Maranzano's hostile attitude immediately following the end of the Castellammarese War. Luciano, always pursuing harmony within the Mafia underworld, had expected a lasting period of peace and prosperity after the antagonistic Masseria was eliminated. However, many mafiosi close to Luciano claimed to hear, directly or through hearsay, that Maranzano was gearing up for yet another large mob conflict. Realizing that the only real competition left to eliminate was himself and his crew, it is likely that Luciano decided sooner rather than later that Maranzano needed dealing with. Whatever the case, Luciano would emerge as the eventual victor, with the faithful and reliable Vito Genovese and Frank Costello as his second-in-command and his personal advisor, respectively.

As much as the early 1930s was a time of great change in Genovese's professional Mafia life, it was also a strange and turbulent time for his personal life. His first wife Donata had died in 1931, and Vito quickly became focused on another woman, Anna Petillo. At the time, Anna was married to a relatively small-time gangster named Gerardo Vernotico. The story surrounding these three individuals is confusing and suspicious. It is unknown whether Genovese truly had a hand in Vernotico's murder, but the facts of the case speak for themselves. Just three months before Genovese and Petillo married, her prior husband was found dead on a New York City rooftop. This was not an ordinary Mafia hit. The circumstances suggest it may have been a crime of passion—Vernotico's body was found bound, brutally beaten, and with a strangling device still around his neck. Police at the time were convinced that Vernotico was tortured. Vito now had himself a new wife. She also just happened to be his distant cousin, for whatever that's worth.

Nineteen thirty-four was another important year for Genovese. Firstly, he moved himself and his new family (which consisted of his new wife, her children, his own children, and eventually their children together) out of Manhattan, which was Vito's main area of operations and which housed his criminal headquarters. Apparently wanting his children to experience life outside "the city," they relocated to a mansion in Middletown Village, one state over in New Jersey. However, he was never too far away from the action, and he kept a second residence in New York City.

In 1932, prohibition ended as a federal law. The Mafia's prime source of income was set to be completely disrupted, and many quickly fell back into their old rackets, such as gambling and prostitution, both of which were relegated as kinds of sideshows during the prohibition era. Genovese himself began running a few scams, including rigged card games. In 1934, a lower level gangster named Ferdinand Boccia, with whom Genovese had had a few negative run-ins already, ran afoul with Genovese and his crew. After organizing a profitable scam for Genovese in order to win the now very powerful mafioso's favor, he began badgering the crew for a cut of the earnings. Frankly, Boccia became an annoyance to Genovese, who had withheld a fair share of the profits from him. So, Genovese resolved to have Boccia killed, and promptly authorized the hit. Boccia was killed in September of 1934. Assassinations were part and parcel of Mafia life and most times, there are little, if any, consequences. But this murder would soon come back to haunt Vito. In 1936, Lucky Luciano, who had been the top Mafia boss since Maranzano's murder, was sent to prison.

Exile

After Luciano was imprisoned, it was his underboss Vito Genovese who was tapped for the role of acting boss. According to the (relatively loose) rules of the Mafia, a boss only lost his position by assassination or abdication—that is, they must die or step down. Since Luciano had done neither, he remained the titular head of the Luciano Family, while his appointee would run the day to day operations. Unfortunately, Genovese would follow in Luciano's footsteps a little too closely. After a surprising streak of good luck and numerous dodged charges, Genovese would have to face the music. Kind of.

With Luciano gone, Dewey turned his attention to Costello and Genovese, the latter of whom was no longer enjoying the high life free of public attention. In fact, it was Dewey who publicly outed the fact that Genovese was the official successor to "Public Enemy Number One," Lucky Luciano, in a case that was pursuing Genovese and a multitude of his companions, including Costello. While the case built against Costello fell flat, it became increasingly likely that Genovese may finally be up against a charge he couldn't escape from: The 1934 murder of Ferdinand Boccia, Genovese's partner in a high level card game scam.

In 1937, just months after he had become a United States citizen, Genovese fled the country to escape from Dewey's crusade. It isn't known exactly when he fled his New Jersey estate for his home country of Italy, but it had to have been before the end of February, when his beloved home in the country burned to the ground under suspicious circumstances. After the blaze had been put out, which involved a grueling, hours-long effort by firefighters, officials said that Genovese was on a European vacation at the time, and had left the furnace running for his entire absence. Nearly nothing was salvageable.

Genovese was apparently accompanied by his wife, who returned home to New York/New Jersey to tend to their several children. Genovese, however, remained in Italy and took residence in his home province of Napoli. By chance, Genovese left on his "vacation" with roughly $750,000 in USD cash, with millions more in credit letters. A man like Genovese would not spend his exile in poverty, of course. Michele Miranda, a co-conspirator with Genovese in Boccia's murder, had also fled for Italy after his own charges were dropped, still fearing Dewey's pursuit. The two men had once again linked up in the old country.

While Genovese was very far from his base of operations and source of income, the Italian political culture at the time presented new, enticing opportunities for willing gangsters. Ironically, the same dictator who had caused a mass exodus of mafiosi from Italy in the 1920s was now in charge of a haven for those fleeing the United States: Benito Mussolini, who had been running the country since 1922. Mussolini still maintained a hardline on Mafia activities officially, even after his 1927 declaration that his Fascists had freed Italy, most notably Sicily, of the Mafia threat. Mussolini, however, was still a politician, and politicians can be relied on to bend the rules and abandon their principles when their situation dictates. The Fascist Italian government needed money, and understood there was plenty to be made in *technically* illegal markets. Genovese, who had soon enmeshed himself in Italy's narcotics trade, wisely believed that if he made himself indispensable to the government, he would be able to operate and thrive within an environment that was incredibly hostile to people like him. Genovese had plenty of starting capital while in Italy, heftily supplemented by routine trips from his wife Anna to deliver more money and his participation in Italian drug trafficking. Mussolini could use that cash.

So it was that Vito Genovese, one of the top mafiosi in the world, had begun to partially fund the Fascist allies of the German Nazis in Italy. Genovese had ingratiated himself with many high level Fascists within the Italian government, including Mussolini himself, as well as his Foreign Minister (and son-in-law) Galeazzo Ciano. It is likely that the latter was even supplied with drugs by Genovese. In return for funding and favors, Genovese was allowed to prosper with top level protection by the Italian government. Genovese was eventually gifted with awards, accolades, and titles by the Italian Fascists. With the threat of a new World War on the horizon, Genovese had at this point fully entrenched himself on the wrong side of history.

Genovese continued to operate after the outbreak of the war. Genovese maintained a cooperative and amicable relationship with Mussolini and his Fascists until it became obviously inexpedient to do so. That point came around summer of 1943. Earlier in the year, a scandal rocked Manhattan. Italian immigrant Carlo Tresca, who had taken residence in the United States nearly two decades before the rise of the Italian Fascists, was gunned down shortly after leaving his Manhattan office. Tresca had operated a socialist weekly publication in Italy and was involved heavily in the unions. In a time where socialists were either looked at with suspicion or actively persecuted around the world, Tresca came to fear that his political dissent and aggressive advocacy would land him in prison. In 1904, he fled the country.

Tresca continued his socialist activism while in the United States, serving as an editor of a prominent Italian-American publication. Of course, socialists and fascists have historically been bitter enemies. After the rise of Mussolini, Tresca began editing an explicitly anti-fascist publication, aptly named *Il Martello*, or "The Hammer," likely a double entendre symbolizing its aggressive rhetoric on the one hand, and a nod to the communist symbol consisting of a hammer and sickle on the other. His work in the United States was well publicized, and he quickly drew the ire of Mussolini. By 1943, while public opinion was already turning against him, Tresca's slander had apparently become a major thorn in the dictator's side.

It is heavily debated what the motivations were for Tresca's murder. But according to many crime historians (and specifically Mafia specialists), it is clear that Genovese used his extensive connections in New York City to arrange for Tresca's murder. The obvious motivation is that Genovese, at the time, was still interested in maintaining the goodwill of Benito "*Il Duce*" Mussolini. A move like this certainly would have placated a megalomaniac like Mussolini, and as far as we know, he and Genovese were still in the other's good graces. But this would soon change.

Mussolini's iron grip on Italy's throat looked less and less sustainable as the middle of 1943 approached. By this point, Italians across the country and abroad were incredibly resentful toward Mussolini over his involvement in World War II. Despite the perceived success of Mussolini's early years in uniting the country under the fascist banner, Italy was still poor. Many people across the country were downtrodden and already exhausted. The last thing those people wanted was a war, which would require the conscription of countless young men. But the political climate at the time demanded Mussolini support his German ally, Adolf Hitler. So, the Italian army was sent to North Africa and the Eastern Front in Russia. Both campaigns were utter disasters, and he had his own people to answer to.

Disaster struck in July of 1943. The United States military, led at the time by famed General George Patton, had landed their invasion forces on the island of Sicily, which lay directly to the south of the Italian mainland. It would take a little over a month for the Italian army to be completely routed, and Sicily came under full control of the Allied forces. But before this could even happen, Italy's Fascist council had held a vote on the leadership capability of Mussolini. The result was troubling for Genovese: The Italian government had lost all confidence in *Il Duce*, Genovese's main protector and ally in Italy. Mussolini was removed from his position at the head of the Italian government and was arrested. He would later be executed and his corpse defaced.

The criminal empire that the Neapolitan boss had built up in Italy was now at risk. But he was an opportunist. With the United States still fighting the war, it is unlikely they would crack down on his narcotics ring any time soon. Still, Genovese was an opportunist, and saw an opening to abandon the Fascist Party and align himself with the obviously soon-to-be victors: The American forces. After the fall of Sicily, the U.S. army quickly moved up the Italian peninsula, reaching the province of Napoli by the Fall of 1943. It took no time at all for Genovese to make his move. The "government" in charge at the time was known as the Allied Military Government of Occupied Territories (AMGOT). AMGOT set up government apparatuses as they marched through enemy territory and took control. In Nola, the Napoli town where he had been operating from, Genovese offered his complete assistance to the local AMGOT office. Genovese was fluent in both Italian and English, and was an American citizen, which made him an attractive ally to be used as an interpreter. AMGOT, which was desperate to control the escalating situation in the city of Napoli and who at the time was completely unaware of who Genovese was, quickly enlisted his help.

Genovese initially served as a liaison between the military government and the people of Napoli, who had been suffering through bombings, food and water shortages, and corrupt politicians. Genovese was apparently responsible for trying to keep the Neapolitan people informed so that they did not revolt or protest, and communicating their grievances to AMGOT. The military government was worried about unrest in the hungry populace, but also worrying was the obvious rise of black market activity. Under Mussolini's reign, it was heavily publicized that the Mafia was dead, and so the surge in racketeering after his downfall was relatively unexpected. Even more unexpected was the fact that they had in their employ perhaps the largest racketeer in Italy at the time. After all, the tendency for mafiosi to carry with them a veneer of professionalism, combined with the fact that the Mafia was thought to be completely irrelevant in Italy, made it surprisingly easy for the United States military officials to be tricked by men like Genovese.

The military eventually began to take the organized crime threat seriously. Their division in charge of sussing out criminal activity within occupied territories was expanded. One of their additions was an intelligence officer named Orange Dickey, who would turn out to be a sort of Dewey-esque crusader in his own right, but with a much smaller scope. Dickey was in charge of investigations in both Napoli and Nola, the latter of which he knew to be an epicenter for underworld activity. The fact that this was Genovese's home was unlikely to be a coincidence. The first successes in the campaign were not against the mafiosi this story is concerned with. Rather, it uncovered dozens of army soldiers, many of whom had been reported AWOL, who had begun turning extra profit by working with local gangsters in the Napoli area. Italians were also arrested. It was these men who would eventually get Dickey onto Genovese's trail.

One of the Italian men picked up in the investigation had apparently named Genovese as the man behind the curtain. Dickey would soon learn of the extent of Genovese's criminal activity in Italy, as well as his highly suspicious relationship with the Mussolini regime. The investigation against Genovese was now in full swing. After a necessary pause in the investigation due to the long awaited eruption of Mount Vesuvius, Dickey got back on track, and through a multitude of informants, had gathered that Genovese had a much longer history of crime than was expected and that he was almost certainly a member of the American Mafia. Dickey was eager to arrest him, despite some apathetic pushback from his superiors. The only problem was that Genovese, once again, could not be found.

In mid-1944, after Genovese had resurfaced briefly to obtain a travel permit, Dickey made his move. He and his men arrested Genovese, and the boss was once again found carrying multiple firearms. His dwelling was later searched, and like Luciano, Genovese's unexplainably expensive tastes would get him into a very messy predicament. A supposedly straight arrow who had been all too willing to lend a hand to the army had no way of justifying living in such opulence while the people of Italy struggled in extreme wartime poverty.

Genovese was now in custody in Italy, but trouble for him was also brewing back home. The Boccia murder investigation, which had been the initial reason Genovese fled in the first place, had been progressing. Around the same time as his arrest in Italy, Genovese had been reliably implicated in the murder. The ball was in Dickey's court, and the staunch investigator began connecting the dots.

Return to New York

It wouldn't be long before Dickey put the pieces together and realized that the man he had in custody for racketeering and weapon charges was the same mafioso who had recently been named in the 1934 murder of Ferdinand Boccia. Dickey had resolved to throw the book at Genovese, and have him shipped back to New York City to face trial. There was considerable resistance from several of the higher ups, however, who did not see the point in expending resources to prosecute or deport Genovese. After all, there was still a war to win, and a volatile domestic situation that threatened to escalate out of control.

Genovese was desperate. He allegedly offered Dickey a quarter of a million dollars to simply listen to his superiors, who had reportedly insisted that Dickey just ignore Genovese. But, Dickey was determined and apparently incorruptible—a mafioso's nightmare. He refused the bribe, ignored his bosses, and continued to press for Genovese's extradition back to NYC. Attempted bribes by Genovese against other army officials yielded similarly disappointing results. Eventually, Dickey's incessant prodding paid off. Genovese was set to be shipped out of Italy to face the U.S. justice system.

Early in June of 1945, Vito Genovese landed in the New York harbor, chaperoned by Orange Dickey himself. Genovese was arraigned the next day for the Boccia murder trial. Genovese also discovered that it was a gangster named Ernie Rupolo. Rupolo had a history with Genovese dating back some years, but Rupolo had issues of his own. Threatened with a murder conviction, Rupolo flipped and implicated Genovese to save himself. His testimony was solid and the prosecution had a pair of reliable witnesses lined up to corroborate Rupolo's damning account. It seemed as though Genovese was finished.

Peter LaTempa and Jerry Esposito were the witnesses set to testify against Genovese upon his return. Unfortunately for Dickey, despite all his best efforts to force Genovese to finally face consequences for his actions, LaTempa and Esposito were both found dead before they could deliver their testimonies. LaTempa was the first to go, found dead in a cell while under police protection. Then in June of 1946, almost exactly a year after Genovese had landed back in New York City, Esposito was found gunned down on a street in New Jersey. Needless to say, the timing and circumstances of both these deaths were highly suspicious. But there was nothing the prosecution could do at the time, pending investigations for both of those murders. For the time being, it was Rupolo's word against Genovese's, and the courts were forced to throw out his case due to a lack of evidence. Yet again, Vito Genovese had slipped through the cracks of the legal system, largely unharmed. He walked free on June 10, 1946.

Genovese was welcomed back into Luciano's Family after his eventful exile in Napoli. However, Costello was not prepared to let Genovese waltz back into New York and reclaim the title of acting boss. This is understandable, as Costello had been faithfully serving Luciano while Genovese lived the high life in Italy, cozying up with dictators and army officials. Willie Moretti, underboss to Costello, was also unwilling to step down for the new returnee. So, Genovese became a *capo*, a hefty demotion for the former acting boss and heir apparent. With Genovese being the man he was, this did not sit well.

While Genovese bided his time, the Mafia world kept rolling. In late 1946, a high-level Mafia meeting was called in Havana, Cuba by Meyer Lansky (under direction from Luciano), who had already established himself in the small island country. Cuban dictator Fulgencio Batista had turned Cuba into a kind of haven for mafiosi, a place where they could operate alongside a friendly government. The island was so enticing that Luciano himself had, earlier in 1946, secretly moved to Cuba from his homeland of Italy where he had been deported after the Second World War. Being barred from the United States, Luciano was also looking to get himself closer to the action and to maintain control over his organization. Cuba, after all, is a mere 90 miles from Florida's southernmost tip.

At the meeting, which came to be dubbed the "Havana Conference" (almost certainly the inspiration for *The Godfather II* Havana meeting called by the fictional Jewish gangster Hyman Roth, who was based off Lansky), Lansky was joined by Luciano, Genovese, Costello, and Anastasia, among others. There were several official issues to be discussed, but Luciano was personally concerned with another matter: Vito Genovese's ambition. Luciano knew well that a man like Genovese would not be satisfied accepting a demotion to a relatively lowly rank. On top of this, Genovese had been antagonizing several other mafiosi by attempting to move in on their territory and expand his own power base. Fearing that Genovese may be gearing up for war, Luciano's secret agenda at the Havana Conference was to reassert himself as the "first among equals" in the Mafia underworld, and to avoid another Castellammarese-style bloody conflict. Genovese had been feuding with Albert Anastasia, boss of the Mangano Family, and to avoid the two factions "going to the mattresses," Luciano heavily insisted that the two gangsters settle their differences then and there. In front of the most powerful Mafia figures in the United States, Genovese begrudgingly shook hands with Anastasia and promised cooperation, officially burying the feud. If Genovese went back on the truce and acted aggressively toward Anastasia now, the concerted Mafia backlash would have been massive. Genovese was forced to temper his ambition. At least for now.

Tension between Genovese and Luciano, however, were at an all-time high. Genovese felt short changed by Luciano and believed he deserved the role of acting Boss in the United States. Luciano, in turn, firmly distrusted Genovese by this point. Near the end of the conference in Havana, Genovese had held a secret meeting with Lucky. Accounts differ on what actually occurred. One story holds that Genovese had urged Luciano to revive the title of *capo di tutti capi* and claim it himself, and allow Genovese to operate the Family in his stead. Other accounts claim that Genovese actually wanted Luciano to simply retire and officially sanction Genovese as the new unquestioned boss of his Family. Some accounts say Luciano calmly but firmly rejected Genovese. Others say Luciano was incensed and lashed out. Supposedly losing his temper, Lucky brutally beat Genovese, breaking his ribs. In any case, he was clearly not ready to hand over the reins to a man he already didn't trust.

Genovese had returned to the United States after the conference and continued operating as the *capo* of his crew. The entire Mafia underworld would soon be coming under heat, however. In 1950, the United States Senate created a committee to investigate organized crime, specifically that which crossed state borders. In the era of The Commission (not to be confused with the Senate committee), this included a great portion of all Mafia activity. It was Democratic Senator from Tennessee, Estes Kefauver, who spearheaded the new committee, and he called on several prominent gangsters to testify at the hearings. Among them were Mickey Cohen, Meyer Lansky, Frank Costello, and his underboss Willie Moretti. The committee also searched relentlessly for Genovese in order to bring him before the court as well, but Genovese had completely eluded the investigators. He knew they were coming for him. There were many successes for law enforcement that came as a result of Kefauver and his committee's work, which will be discussed in later chapters. For now, what is important is that Willie Moretti, a big player in the Luciano Family, delivered a testimony that was less than satisfactory, at least as far The Commission was concerned.

Nearly every gangster called to testify at the Kefauver Hearings remained silent, repeatedly refusing to answer the committee's questions. Moretti was the notable exception. Costello also appeared visibly nervous, but did not offer much information that could be considered damning. Seemingly co-operating with the committeemen, Moretti was comparatively very responsive when asked direct questions. More than this, he seemed to be inexplicably enjoying himself. He frequently told jokes and made light of the situation, in stark contrast to most of the other mafiosi's stoic silence. His strange behavior was a cause for concern among Genovese Family leadership, Genovese included. The Family knew that Moretti had syphilis, and had already begun to fear that it was progressing into his brain. After seeing how he conducted himself at the Kefauver Hearings in 1950-51, something had to be done about Costello's underboss before he completely lost his inhibitions and began spilling secrets to anyone who would ask him.

The Moretti situation called for action by The Commission. The governing body quickly authorized his murder, and placed an open contract on his head. In the Fall of 1951, Moretti was at a New Jersey restaurant with a group of friends. The identities of these men is not entirely certain, though they were likely Albert Anastasia's men. The official story is that they were the only patrons in the restaurant at the time, and when the waitress had walked out, leaving the men alone inside the dining room, shots were heard and Moretti was found shot to death by his table. Moretti was alone, and his companions, who were almost certainly the shooters, had fled before either the restaurant staff or law enforcement could see them. A gangster named John Robliotto was eventually picked up for the crime, but the case against him collapsed.

Two more issues preoccupied Genovese. First, he and his wife Anna were going through a serious rough patch. Anna had for years been assisting Genovese in his criminal activity, and allegedly even ran some of his operations while he was exiled in Italy. This was on top of the regular trips she made to deliver money to her husband while he was away. Something, however, had changed for her. While Genovese was apparently still deeply in love with her, Anna had apparently grown to resent Genovese, and after they had been separated, Anna filed for divorce.

What ensued was a messy battle between the two, with Anna publicly testifying about Genovese's personal life and his alleged extramarital affairs. Genovese and his team had called in their own witnesses to try to debunk Anna's "wild" claims, but the damage was done. Criminal activity was brought up during the couple's spat, and in the aftermath of the Kefauver Hearings, the last thing the Mafia needed was more public attention drawn to it. This bizarre detour in Genovese's life, which finally calmed down by 1954, irked many other mafiosi, who apparently were aghast at him for letting his personal marriage crisis become a sensational news story.

Second, Genovese was once again at risk of deportation, this time back to Italy. As part of the government's crackdown on organized crime, and because mafiosi were so often difficult to nail down, they tried their hand at a new strategy. Since many prominent Mafia figures were only naturalized American citizens, not by birth, there was still a possibility of deportation. This way, the legal system wouldn't have to go through the cumbersome process of charging and trying the oft-slippery gangsters and attempting to round up reliable witnesses before hitmen got to them first, only to have the charges thrown out after months of work. But how could they deport American citizens? Only if they were never *legitimately* citizens in the first place.

Government agents began poring over the history and backgrounds of some of their top Mafia targets, trying to find any evidence that they had falsified their documents for naturalization. Since one of the earliest Mafia activities in the United States was counterfeiting immigration papers, the idea that some of these men would lie on their own documents was by no means a stretch. Genovese was one of their primary targets, and as it happens, Genovese did in fact lie on his naturalization papers. He had claimed on his documents that he had never been convicted of a crime, which was known to be false. He also saw fit to omit his nearly 10 previous arrests. This was grounds for the revocation of citizenship and eventual deportation.

Genovese was eventually summoned to court to explain himself in the Winter of 1954. The goal of the prosecution was simple: Prove that Genovese *intentionally* lied on his citizenship documents. Genovese would be hard pressed to maintain that he had never been arrested or charged prior to signing the papers, so his strategy instead was to convince the court that he, at the time, did not believe that he was lying or falsifying the documents. He frequently gave vague and sometimes contradictory answers to the court's questions. He also claimed that the government officials who facilitated his citizenship application had apparently not even asked Genovese about minor crimes or arrests, only felony convictions. Because of the hastily completed work of the officials, Genovese maintained that if his documents were in fact invalid, it was the fault of the care-free government employee, not himself. Of course, Vito Genovese would never want to lie to the government.

The court was evidently not convinced. Genovese lost his American citizenship despite his best efforts. While this did not necessarily mean that he would get deported (and if he would, it would take quite some time for that process to play out), it was certainly worth being concerned about. The man who seemingly had a guardian angel protecting him from the consequences of his actions was perhaps now more vulnerable than ever. At least in the short term, however, Genovese continued expanding his power and influence.

Costello had bigger problems than Genovese. He spent some time in prison resulting from a contempt of Congress conviction, was facing a potential loss of citizenship like Genovese, and had lost a number of his key allies to death or deportation, notably underboss Willie Moretti. He was also being actively investigated for income fraud at the time. Given his unstable position, Genovese saw a window of opportunity.

In May of 1957, Genovese sent Vincent Gigante, a man we will return to later, to kill Costello. He was shot in the head, but Gigante's aim was off and the target survived with a flesh wound. At the same time, Genovese and his faction were preparing for war, knowing full well that the attempt on Costello could cause massive backlash. But the response was surprisingly quiet. Rather than start a new mob war, Costello decided to quietly retire. He handed over reins to Genovese, who had at long last become boss of the Luciano Crime Family, formerly the Morello Family, formerly the 107th Street Mob.

Around the same time, Genovese had been active in a separate plot. Albert Anastasia was the current Boss of the Mangano Family and was a long-time friend of both Luciano and Costello. It is likely that Genovese began plotting against Anastasia in an attempt to further weaken Costello and his alliance network. One of Anastasia's men, Carlo Gambino, was a respected gangster and friend of Genovese. This presented an opportunity, and Genovese's proposal was simple: Kill Anastasia and have the friendlier Gambino take power. The two agreed, and in the Fall of 1957, Anastasia was shot dead in a barbershop, leaving Gambino the clear successor.

Things were looking very up for Genovese in 1957. He was now the head of arguably the most powerful Mafia Family in the country, and had a close ally working alongside him as boss of his own Family. It seemed that two-fifths of New York's Mafia structure were now working in tandem, with the Luciano and Mangano Families headed by two aspirational and ruthless gangsters who would both eventually name their respective Families after themselves. Genovese certainly had some profitable years ahead, but although his position as boss would last over a decade, his time as a free man was soon to expire.

Caught at Last

After Genovese had taken control of the Luciano Family, he sought to consolidate his power. The first thing to do was to publicly (to the Mafia underworld) assert his dominance, just as Luciano had done years earlier in Havana. To that end, Genovese called for a meeting of national Mafia figures, and Pennsylvania boss Joe Barbara was entrusted to make the arrangements. The meeting took place in November of 1957 at Barbara's home in the New York town of Apalachin. There were several pressing issues to be officially discussed, but Genovese's motive was clear enough. Unfortunately for Genovese, rather than entrench his grip on the American Mafia, the Apalachin meeting tarnished his respectability. Barbara took great pains to avoid information about the meeting leaking to law enforcement before it took place. He was largely successful, but a fatal mistake was made. One of the cheques used to reserve a motel room for one of the numerous gangsters flying into New York was bad. Owners called police who by chance discovered that known mafioso Barbara had reserved a number of rooms for unnamed men. The story given to the owners was that the guests were flying in for a convention. The police became suspicious after inspecting the supposed venue and finding barely any activity. So, police decided to check out Barbara's home instead, and what they stumbled into was a clandestine meeting of the most powerful criminals in North America.

Shockingly, no arrests came after police broke up the meeting and caught several of the fleeing gangsters. Almost none of them had brought weapons with them, and the ones who did had permits. None had arrest warrants at the time, and all had their alibi prepared: They had organized a visit for their sick friend, Barbara. Police let all the men go free, but the mob leaders were not at all happy. They feared that yet another exposition of the Mafia in the national spotlight would bring even more unwanted attention from law enforcement. They were right to be angry at Genovese: The Apalachin incident caused a flurry of media headlines and opened the window for more police investigations.

Things would quickly get worse for Genovese. In 1958 he was arrested on drug trafficking charges. At the time, law enforcement was aggressively pursuing drug distribution in the country. Additionally, both the Kefauver Hearings and Vito and Anna's marital spat had hinted at the fact that the Mafia, and Genovese in particular, were involved in the drug trade. At some point prior to the arrest, Genovese and some of his men became entangled in a narcotics scheme, which law enforcement either had known was taking place or found out soon after. Allegedly, it was Carlo Gambino who masterminded the plot, along with Tommy Lucchese as his partner. Gambino supposedly leveraged his friendship with Genovese to eliminate the Neapolitan Don for good.

The plot theory has been heavily debated, however if it is true, it is likely that Gambino and company sanctioned it for two reasons: Gambino was attempting to muscle in on Genovese's territory, and many at the time believed that Genovese should be punished for his role in the Apalachin incident. Whatever the case, Genovese was finally convicted on a solid charge, and received a 15 year sentence in 1959. There are several unanswered questions surrounding Genovese's conviction. Namely, the fact that the prosecution alleged that the boss was *personally* involved in the drug exchange. Frankly, this would have been incredibly unlikely. Mafia bosses take great pains to insulate themselves from crimes, and there is no reason that the trial against him should have been as easy as it was. If it's true that there was a conspiracy, it is almost certain that the witnesses called to testify were paid to do so. All of this mattered little to Genovese, however, who was now in prison where he would remain until his death in 1969.

Chapter 5:

The Road to the RICO Act

After Vito Genovese was locked up, he would remain the titular Boss of the Genovese Family for about a decade. In his absence, however, the higher ups in the Family formed a council, or a kind of *junta*, to make decisions on Genovese's behalf and to run the day-to-day operations of the organization. The first of these councils consisted of the current acting boss Tommy Eboli, his underboss Gerardo Catena, and Philip Lombardo, also known as "Benny Squint," a nickname earned for his thick eyeglasses and reportedly terrible vision. The Family continued operating in this fashion through the 1960s, however by 1970, the Mafia world would be irreparably shaken by the passing of the Racketeer Influenced and Corrupt Organizations Act, also known as RICO. This chapter will detail the story of the RICO Act as well as the American Mafia's struggles to adapt in a world that grew more hostile all the time.

The Valachi Hearings and the End of *Omerta*

In 1959, Genovese mafioso Joe Valachi was sent to prison alongside Genovese, both men being served with 15 years. The pair ended up at the same prison in Atlanta where they were reportedly bunkmates for a time. They got along amicably at the beginning and looked out for each other. But with each passing day in prison, Valachi grew more paranoid. He believed that Genovese was beginning to turn against him and suspected other prisoners of attempting to persuade the boss to get rid of Valachi. In addition to this, Valachi later reported that Genovese talked with him on several occasions about how rats in the Mafia needed to be weeded out and eliminated. The mobster's paranoia had convinced him that these were coded threats, and that Genovese was referring to Valachi as the rat that needed weeding out. This came to a head in 1962 when Valachi beat a fellow prisoner to death, suspecting that he was a hitman sent by Genovese.

Now facing murder charges in addition to narcotics, Valachi faced the possibility of spending the rest of his life in prison. A terrified Valachi had decided that his best option was to offer his full cooperation with the government. Prison with Genovese simply wasn't safe. In October of 1963, Valachi delivered a testimony to the Senate that would change Mafia culture forever. He detailed the history of the Mafia, his own day-to-day operations as a soldier, Family structure, crimes, and even named certain prominent gangsters.

For the first time in American history, a Made Man officially acknowledged the existence of the American Mafia to outsiders, on public record. He named all Five Families and who their Bosses were. Not even the half insane Willie Moretti told courts this. He even detailed the esoteric induction rituals, perhaps the most mysterious aspect of Mafia culture. These hearings brought an intense amount of scrutiny on the American Mafia, and *Cosa Nostra* had become a famous term almost overnight. Finally, the Mafia was not a secret. In many ways, 1963 was the end of *omerta*.

The Kefauver committee were the oil-soaked rags, and the Valachi hearings were the spark. The era after Valachi saw a sharp rise in the efforts of various government officials to crack down on organized crime, and renewed the image of the Mafia in public consciousness. The old ways of living in the shadows would not work anymore, and organized crime had to adapt. Criminals and cops were in an arms race, and RICO was on the horizon.

The Crusaders

There were many important individuals involved with the task of destroying the Mafia, many of which have already been discussed. By the time of the Apalachin meeting, however, there were crusaders emerging at some of the highest levels of government. Among them was the famous and long-time Director of the FBI: J. Edgar Hoover. He had been Director since the FBI's inception in 1935 until his death in 1972. It was a monumental career, but it was not without its controversies. For roughly the first three decades, Hoover hadn't made any noteworthy progress on Mafia activity and insisted that organized crime wasn't a concern.

But why? There are two hints. Several sources have claimed that the Mafia had been blackmailing Hoover for decades with images, allegedly obtained by Costello and Lansky, showing Hoover behaving in a highly suggestive manner with another male, his Deputy Clyde Tolson. It's also very likely that Hoover didn't want to crackdown because he himself was involved with the Mafia. It's known that Hoover was a habit gambler and liked playing the races. It has been alleged that Hoover received tip offs on fixed games by Mafia officials, a gift for looking the other way.

Whatever the case, Hoover spared gangsters federal heat for decades. This would change with the 1957 Apalachin disaster and the 1963 Valachi hearings. After these events, the FBI received heavy criticism for its lax attitude. It was no longer politically tenable for Hoover to ignore the Mafia, and now, organized crime would have the full force of national investigators to contend with from the 1960s onwards.

In 1961, Robert Kennedy was appointed Attorney General of the United States. After the Kefauver hearings, Kennedy was incensed by the power of organized crime. His objectives as Attorney General were clear to everyone: Destroy the Mafia and remove their influence from unions, specifically the Teamsters. His prior work included numerous investigations into Teamsters president Jimmy Hoffa, who had fully enmeshed his union with the Mafia. After Valachi, Kennedy's resolve was hardened and remained unshaken until tragedy struck his family about a month later. His brother, President John Kennedy, was assassinated in a Dallas motorcade. As himself and the nation mourned, his crusade took a backseat, but it would not be long before he continued his puritanical investigation before his own assassination in 1968.

Because of the involvement with the Mafia, conspiracies swirl around the Kennedy murders to this day. Many believe that the President was assassinated on Mafia orders in order to send a message to Robert that his crusade was unwelcome. Even Robert's assassination was rumored to be a Mafia hit. If these conspiracies are true, they would absolutely be the boldest actions taken in Mafia history. While there is precedence for Mafia involvement in extremely high level assassinations (several mafiosi had been enlisted by the U.S. government in the wake of the Cuban Revolution to attempt to assassinate new Presidente Fidel Castro), there is very little to support this theory.

Even if the Mafia didn't take such drastic actions, there's no doubt that both Hoover and Kennedy had become serious issues for organized crime. The mission that Thomas Dewey had invigorated in the 1930s and 1940s was being carried into the second half of the 20th century by a new, more well-equipped generation of agents. Though Kennedy would die before his work culminated with RICO, his efforts would have devastating consequences for the Families in the 1970s and 1980s, when another new crusader, lawyer Rudolf Giuliani, entered the fray.

The Era of "Front Bosses"

With the threat of FBI investigations intensifying and with new, high-profile figures waging public campaigns against them, the Mafia was forced to adapt or die. The system which the Genovese Family had developed over decades to insulate high-level figures from prosecution had to be refined, as it was already clear that the system was not watertight. The apparent solution was to do what they did best: Deception. The system of "Front Bosses" was developed.

It was simple: A selected member of the Family would act like the boss. They would carry themselves as the boss, subordinates would treat them like the boss, and they would serve as the face of the Family. The obvious intent was to sow confusion and misdirection among investigators and to throw them off the scent of Philip Lombardo, the man who would take over the Family after Genovese died in prison in 1969. Eboli, who likely would have become boss were it not for his poor health, served as the first front boss until his murder three years later.

Sometime in the late 1960s, Eboli had taken a loan from the Gambino Family to fund new rackets. After his operation had been quashed by law enforcement, Eboli was clearly unable to repay the debt, infuriating Carlo Gambino. The matter was taken to The Commission, and after deliberation, the hit on Eboli was sanctioned. In July of 1972, the front boss was murdered in a drive by shooting. Carmine Zeccardi would briefly fill in as Lombardo's mask before his disappearance.

Genovese Family *capo* Frank Tieri was next up. It is rumored that Gambino actually planned this, desiring the diplomatic and friendly Tieri in charge of the (at times) rival Genoveses. If true, then even the other New York Families were fooled—Lombardo, not Tieri, was the one calling the real shots. With this front boss system in place, the FBI had essentially been chasing false leads for nearly 20 years straight. It worked: Lombardo, the first Genovese boss protected by front bosses, escaped prosecution for his tenure, and retired peacefully in 1981. He later died a free man six years later. The front bosses themselves proved not nearly as fortunate in the era of RICO.

Vincent Gigante, who will be discussed more shortly, further renovated the front boss system when he became the head of the Genoveses. They would receive more responsibilities and more drawn heat. The ever-paranoid Gigante needed not only men who would be boss on paper, but men who literally had to take to the streets and do his job for him. As will be discussed, Gigante's fear of leaving his home would seriously interfere with the Genovese Family structure and chain of command.

The RICO Act

In 1970, the Racketeer Influenced and Corrupt Organizations Act, also known as RICO, was passed into law after being drafted by Robert Blakey and Senator John McClellan. The latter was the same man who oversaw the Valachi hearings. RICO was primarily intended to deal a death blow to the American Mafia by attacking one of their most valuable tools: Their assets. Often, when top Mafia figures were at risk of conviction, their assets would be liquidated to eliminate the possibility of prosecutors seizing anything of value. Sometimes they would be transferred into safer hands, and also would be funneled into their legal team's defense fund so as to secure a reliable and experienced group of lawyers to fight on their behalf. Cash would also sometimes be used to fund the hits on key witnesses, ensuring that the prosecution team would have little corroboration.

Under RICO, prosecutors were able to place temporary seizures on all Mafia assets and cash believed to have been acquired through racketeering. This was possible even *before* the trial began, ensuring that gangsters couldn't put up the money for open hit contracts, afford lawyers, or stash away their money and assets in safer locations outside the reach of the law. This was instrumental to law enforcement, as the inability to pay for a legal team forced many gangsters over the following decades to simply plead guilty or to accept bargaining agreements.

For those facing potential RICO charges, the penalties would be stiff. Individuals found to have committed two or more racketeering crimes in a 10 year span in service of an overall criminal enterprise could face large fines and 20 years in prison *per count*. In the case of the Mafia, the "enterprise" obviously referred to the organized Mafia Family unit. Since, by this point, the government and American public were already largely aware of the existence of the Mafia, the association of criminals with Mafia Families was not a difficult task. The number of crimes listed as applicable racketeering charges was large, and after some time, RICO proved highly effective. After only two years, a majority of states in the U.S. adopted their own state level RICO laws to further inhibit interstate crime.

After nine years, the first RICO trial took place. Interestingly, it was not levied against any members of the American Mafia, but rather against a gang of burglars in California and Nevada. They had apparently conducted themselves in a way that the courts deemed close enough to organized crime. For many years after the passing of RICO, the upper strata of the Mafia hierarchy would be relatively untouched. But beginning in the 1980s, federal prosecutors would begin gunning for the Genovese Crime Family.

Chapter 6:

Vincent "The Chin" Gigante and the 1980s

The 1980s was a time of turmoil, uncertainty, and paranoia for the Genovese Family and the Mafia at large. RICO had already proven effective in the 1970s, but the true test would be capturing Mafia bosses. Still, nothing seemed to stop the Mafia machinery from chugging along, and the Genovese Family was looking forward to new opportunities and potentially more freedom for the higher ups as long as their Front Boss ruse kept up. This chapter will detail the Genovese Family in the 1980s as well as the rise of former lowly enforcer, Vincent Gigante.

Expansion

One of the first major steps for the Genoveses in the 1980s was to attempt to expand. Four years earlier, Atlantic City had legalized gambling and casino operations. Atlantic City was not much to look at at the time, but the Philadelphia-based Bruno Family seized the opportunity. Bruno man Nico Scarfo was sent there to run gambling operations on behalf of the Family. Scarfo quickly made a name for himself, and after his company was contracted to build several casinos, he massively grew his powerbase from his casino involvement. He was the big man in Atlantic City.

Meanwhile, Antonio Caponigro, *consigliere* to boss Angelo Bruno, was plotting. He had believed that Bruno's time had come and desired to run the powerful Philadelphia Family himself. Caponigro reached out to the Genovese Family in New York, wanting to strike a deal with current (front) boss Frank Tieri. Some sources claim the opposite: Tieri lured Caponigro into the plot. In any case, the agreement was successful: Caponigro felt secure in his decision to have Bruno eliminated, apparently being assured by Tieri that he would receive support by the Mafia Commission. Tieri had different plans, however, and never intended on informing the Commission of the plans, nor to support Caponigro in the aftermath. In March of 1980, Bruno was gunned down outside his house in Philly.

It's not fully clear how The Commission knew Caponigro was behind the plot. Regardless, he was called to explain himself. At the meeting, it was alleged that Tieri denied any knowledge of the plan and supported the decision to condemn the Pennsylvania *consigliere*. The Commission ruled that it was a rogue hit on a protected boss. Caponigro's body was discovered the next month.

The death of two of the Bruno Family's highest ranking members resulted in a bloody struggle for power in Philadelphia. The Genovese Family, headed by the Lombardo/Tieri duo, threw their weight behind Nico Scarfo, the big time Atlantic City gambling lord who was looking to claim power from his now deceased superiors in Philly. In the end, Scarfo was successful, ushering in a new era for the Bruno Family. In exchange for the support, the Genoveses were granted the blessing of Scarfo to operate in the Atlantic City gambling industry, upon which he maintained an iron grip.

The Genovese's meddling in the affairs of distant Families was successful, but while the Philadelphia affair played out, trouble struck for the Family. Frank Tieri had been brought to court on racketeering charges as part of an ongoing criminal enterprise. Tieri was sick and weak by this point, and his lawyers used this to their advantage, attempting to leverage his condition for a lesser sentence. The courts didn't fall for it, and Tieri was convicted at the beginning of 1981, becoming the first Mafia boss in history to be convicted on a RICO charge, beginning an era of fear for organized crime. As it happens, Tieri had not been faking his sickness: Barely two months after being sent to prison, the front boss succumbed to his ailments and died in captivity.

After Tieri went away, the new appointed front boss was Tony Salerno. This was not the only shakeup in the Family: Philip Lombardo, the man running the Family from behind the curtain, decided to retire, leaving the failed Costello assassin, Vincent Gigante, in charge of the Family.

Vincent "The Chin" Gigante

Vincent Gigante was a brutish, dim-looking man with an imposing figure, who had acquired the nickname "The Chin" for his rather large facial feature. Having been a boxer in the 1940s, Gigante began his Mafia career as an enforcer for and apprentice of Vito Genovese. He was just a teenager when he linked up with the Mafia crowd, and had racked up an extensive rap sheet before he even reached 26 years old. However, much like his mentor Genovese, Gigante would largely avoid any significant jail time. After entrenching himself as a Made Man in the Genovese Family, Gigante cut his teeth in union racketeering, as well as predatory lending and gambling operations. He also was a trusted button man for Genovese, and carried out high profile hits, like the seminal attempt on Boss Frank Costello's life.

Though Gigante's Genovese-ordered hit on Frank Costello would be a monumental failure, he remained a trusted member of the Family for decades. Gigante would escape conviction for attempted murder because of Costello's adherence to *omerta*, but he wouldn't be as lucky in 1959, during the same trial that sent Genovese away until his death. Gigante, however, would serve only five years and would in fact be promoted after his release. He was again charged in 1969 on a bribery accusation, however his charges were dropped when his legal team pointed to his poor mental health as a mitigating factor. This idea that Gigante was mentally unstable would become a theme for him for the rest of his life, regardless of whether or not he truly was ill.

By the time Gigante took the reins from Philip Lombardo, the Genovese Family was no longer the obviously most powerful crime organization in New York. The Gambinos, often at odds with the Genoveses, had built a powerful rival Family, and would soon be headed by one of the most famous gangsters in history: John Gotti. Gotti had ordered the murder of previous Gambino boss, Paul Castellano, who had been a friend of Gigante. Further complicating matters was that the Castellano hit was apparently unsanctioned by the Mafia Commission. Gotti seized power, and the hit began a tense rivalry between the two bosses that would come to a head in 1986, just months after Castellano's unauthorized murder.

There were a few key moments which greatly affected the ability of Gigante to rule the Family in this new era. The first had come before he even took power. In 1981, the government had convicted their first Mafia Boss under RICO: Frank Tieri. Gigante, already a strange man, became paranoid at the thought of indictment. A number of prominent RICO indictments were made throughout the 1980s, including Gigante's friend, Gambino leader Paul Castellano, in 1984. These indictments would only strengthen his psychosis. Then, in Spring of 1992, John Gotti himself was hit with a RICO conviction after his arrest two years earlier. Gotti received terrifying news: He was handed down a life sentence for his crimes.

Gigante was perpetually afraid that he would be next, and took drastic, unusual measures to ensure his safety. Frankly, he became a hermit. Terrified of being followed or spied on, he rarely left his home. When he had to, he ensured that the house was never unoccupied, fearing that federal agents would sneak in to plant wiretaps or other listening devices. He was known to whisper when speaking to people to avoid his voice being picked up by any potential bugs, and only made phone calls as a last resort. He reportedly would even bang or blow into the phone before speaking to annoy and deter any would-be eavesdroppers. Genovese men had to rely on hand gestures or cryptonyms to refer to Gigante—they were instructed to never utter his name.

Gigante was thoroughly paranoid, a product of the circumstances at the time and the meltingly hot light that federal prosecutors had placed the Mafia under. Things would be getting worse for Gigante and the rest of the Mafia halfway through the decade, however. Organized crime was up against a hefty new investigation, and this one would strike at the highest level of American organized crime: The Mafia

Commission. Leading the 1985 indictments was a new up-and-coming anti-Mafia crusader by the name Rudolph Giuliani.

Rudy Giuliani and the Mafia Trials

Before the Mafia Commission Trial, which would make him a prominent national figure, Giuliani already had an impressive history. Around the same time as his graduation from Law School in Manhattan, Giuliani became more involved in politics. The first campaign he was a part of was the 1968 Presidential run of Robert Kennedy, the premier anti-mob crusader of the time. He would later work in the administration of Gerald Ford and in the early 1980s became Ronald Reagan's associate attorney general. In 1983 he became the U. S. attorney for New York's Southern District, where he personally prosecuted criminals and racked up an extensive list of convictions. Giuliani had earlier focused on prosecuting corruption within the American government itself, but by the early 1980s, he had set his sights on New York's organized criminal underworld.

With the expressed goal of destroying the empires that the Mafia had built in his city over decades, Giuliani set to work on a set of indictments which would come to be known as the Mafia Commission Trial, held between 1985 and 1986. Earlier in the decade, New York's special task force unit for organized crime had learned of the Mafia Commission and its internal workings through surveillance and wiretaps. This presented a wonderful opportunity for prosecutors. Before, courts could use RICO to attack the vertical structure of a particular crime Family (for example, linking a Bonanno Family boss with crimes of a Bonanno Family soldier, etc.), but now they could prosecute horizontally across the Mafia leadership board by connecting them all within the ongoing criminal entity of The Commission, of which they were all a part. The possibility of the Mafia leadership being decimated in one fell strike was now on the table. Vincent Gigante was right to be paranoid.

The Commission Trial began in February of 1985 and would not close until the end of 1986. Nearly a dozen Mafia figures from New York's

Families received indictments ranging from union corruption to murder and assassination plots. All pleaded not guilty, and all but two were convicted. The only two who escaped their convictions were the Gambino boss and underboss, Paul Castellano and Aniello Dellacroce. But they were not exactly free men; Castellano had been murdered before facing conviction, and Dellacroce succumbed to his cancer. Bonanno boss Phil Rastelli, another defendant, was sentenced under a separate trial. All of the other eight surviving defendants received sentences of 100 years in federal prison, with the only exception being one of Rastelli's *capos*, who received only 40 years.

The convictions resulted in the destruction of several of the New York Families' leadership structures. The Lucchese and Colombo Families were particularly hard hit, with the former losing the top three highest ranking members of leadership, including boss Tony Corallo. Although the number of life sentences handed down to high ranking bosses vindicated Vincent Gigante's psychosis, he was not one of the defendants on trial. Because, of course, he was not the official boss of the Family. It was instead Tony Salerno, the front boss, who would be sent away for the rest of his life.

As far as Giuliani was concerned, he had just sent the head of the Genovese Family away to prison for a century. But he, just like government prosecutors for a decade and a half before him, had been fooled by the front boss ruse. The true leader was safe, operating the Family from his self-imposed isolation. But, despite the greatest of pains that Gigante took to make himself scarce and hidden away from the FBI, the scheme that saved him from the Commission Trial was soon to be exposed, and with it, the identity of the true boss.

In March of 1986, Genovese man Vincent Cafaro was indicted. He was set to be put away for his role in organizing labor union racketeering, but before he faced trial, he took a drastic step to avoid prison. Drastic, but by this point, common. He reached out to federal prosecutors and offered his services as a witness against the Mafia. He was the latest in a long line of mafiosi-turned-witnesses, a line which had grown exponentially since the testimony of Joe Valachi. Cafaro provided the government with information on the structure of the Family and the details of their criminal activity. He even secretly recorded meetings between Family officials. Most importantly, he revealed that when prosecutors sent away the boss of the Genovese Family for 100 years, they had the wrong guy. Salerno was revealed as a simple figurehead boss for Vincent "The Chin" Gigante, a gangster known for his erratic behavior and history of apparent mental illness. The front boss scheme was now exposed, likely to the embarrassment of the FBI, who were informed by Salerno that they had been hoodwinked since 1969, nearly two decades.

The Downfall of Gigante

Though Gigante was now a clear target for the FBI, he would not face consequences until the 1990s. Since at least the late 1970s, the Family had been involved in monopolizing window installation contracts in New York City. Having the installation companies whose unions were controlled by the Genoveses get a majority of contracts was a clear benefit to the Family, who received payouts according to union labor. This task involved rigging the system put in place to award contracts to different companies: Price bidding. Unsurprisingly, prices for contracts rose dramatically as a result of Mafia infestation in bid controlling.

In May of 1990, the shut-in Gigante was finally indicted for his role and leadership in this union racketeering operation. In the era of RICO, it is likely that Gigante was going to receive a harsh sentence. This would have been especially concerning to him after seeing a great number of his colleagues sent away for life by Rudolph Giuliani just a few years prior. Gigante and his legal team decided to use a tactic that had proved useful in the Boss' past. They plead insanity and claimed the mafioso was not in the proper state of mind to conduct himself in a criminal trial. Mental help is what he needed, not prison. This was an image that Gigante had kept up for some time, and to quell any doubts, he attended his arraignment "in his customary street garb: Pajamas and a bathrobe" (Raab, 2005). He was looking disheveled and confused.

While it is not out of the question that Gigante truly had mental impairments, it is widely believed that this was all a trick. The idea of mobsters pleading insanity to avoid prison became a sort of cliche after this spectacle, even being referenced in HBO's *The Sopranos*, when the

Family's aging boss faced his own criminal charges. Regardless of whether Gigante's mental health struggles were genuine, the 1990 indictment would get tied up for years over whether or not Gigante could legally be brought before a court. It didn't matter much, however, as he would have more issues to deal with before a resolution would be reached.

In 1992, the unofficial current *capo di tutti capi* John Gotti, head of the powerful Gambinos, was convicted after being implicated in several murder charges. This high profile conviction put Gigante even more on edge, because with Gotti gone, he was now in charge of arguably the most influential crime organization in New York. He was a big target. In the Summer of the following year, Gigante received a fresh set of indictments, this time for his involvement in murder and attempted murder. One of the charges was levied against him for his alleged ordering of the failed hit on Gotti in the late 1980s, a retaliatory measure for Castellano's death. For what it's worth, this was at least Gigante's second botched hit.

Gigante's legal team acquired numerous testimonies which corroborated the story of the boss' mental incapacity, but it would be in vain. Earlier in the 1990s, former Gambino underboss Sam Gravano flipped and became a witness for the government. About five years later he was called to Gigante's 1996 hearing to help demystify the boss' mental state. Unfortunately for Gigante, Gravano told the prosecutors exactly what they wanted to hear. According to him, Gigante was a perfectly sane and rational man, and had been for years. Of course, if he wasn't he never would have been able to organize and lead one of the largest criminal enterprises in the country. Along with the front boss scheme, insanity was simply another tool to conceal the paranoid Gigante from the prying eyes and ears of the FBI and federal prosecutors. This was enough to convince the courts that he was fit to stand trial. Another key witness for the government was Peter Savino, a mobster whom Gigante had apparently actually trusted, uncharacteristic of a man stricken with paranoia. In the Winter of 1997, Vincent "The Chin" Gigante was convicted and handed a 12 year sentence. Though this was still possibly a life sentence for the aging and ailing Gigante, the boss got off surprisingly easy.

Gigante now joined a long line of infamous Genovese bosses put behind bars. Despite his conviction, Gigante would remain the titular head of the Genoveses into the 21st century. But the persecution of Italian-American organized crime, which had already done irreparable damage to Mafia structures and organization, would continue to menace all five of New York's crime Families. The year 2000 was the start of yet another new decade of federal investigations, one that would result in a considerable disruption within the Family that Gigante had run from prison. This will be the focus of the next chapter.

Chapter 7:

Mafia in the New Millennium

Gigante's conviction was certainly not the last blow to be dealt to the Genoveses by the feds. From the late 1990s into the new millennium, it seemed as though the once-elusive Family faced a never-ending onslaught of indictments and convictions. Eventually the Genoveses were left broken and confused, having to piece themselves back together after disruption of their leadership structure. Nevertheless, the Genoveses persisted and continue to operate even today.

The Chin in Prison

The Mafia, and the Genovese Family in particular, have a history of being run by bosses who were imprisoned. Generally, runners would visit the incarcerated boss and relay information, orders, and recommendations back to the acting boss, or in some cases, a ruling panel or council. Vito Genovese and Lucky Luciano had both done it. In earlier decades, it was a relatively simple task for a Family to continue to operate under an imprisoned man. Prisons were more lenient toward organized crime, and it was generally easy to bribe the right people to give themselves wiggle room. You may recall the scene from Martin Scorsese's film *Goodfellas*, where Henry Hill and company are sent to prison, where they lived like kings, enjoying their time and patiently waiting for their release. This is a dramatization, but not fully removed from the truth.

Perhaps Gigante was simply a victim of his times. He became Boss during a time of intense hostility toward the Mafia, and it was even worse by the time he was sent to prison. So, continuing to run the Family from behind bars would prove to be a challenge for Gigante in the late 1990s and early 2000s. Imprisoned gangsters were monitored heavily during their interactions with strangers, and so for many, running messages wasn't feasible—those who tried often had their runners end up in prison with them. Gigante, however, managed to keep tabs on and remain in communication with the Family via Andrew Gigante, his son. This lasted for about five years, until the Genovese command structure had taken another serious hit. A good deal of Gigante's captains had been either imprisoned or murdered by this point, and some of the aging and trusted veterans were suffering health complications. With the boss out of communication and with the loss of his most trusted guys on the outside, the Genovese Family was in a crisis.

In 2002, Gigante faced yet another charge for criminal actions *while in prison*. He was joined in his indictment by his son, Andrew—the government had discovered that Gigante was still running the Genoveses from within their prison. Another Gigante charade was exposed, and he was responsible for his own son now facing decades in prison. With things looking very bad for the boss, he decided to admit he was guilty. He told prosecutors much of what they wanted to hear about his crimes to strike a deal.

While it had long been accepted that mafiosi were prone to flipping for the government when facing conviction, a boss of a Family cooperating with the government was a brutal shock. Even Genovese front boss Salerno, who was sent to prison for life in order to keep Gigante out, did not break *omerta*. It is likely that Gigante, losing access to the Family he had run since 1981, felt he had nothing left to lose. To his credit, however, part of the deal he struck with the government was to keep his son, who had also been involved in the Family, out of prison. Andrew was still convicted, but his sentence was a fraction of what it would have been without Gigante's plea.

Prior to the trial, Gigante had discovered the evidence that the prosecution intended on submitting to the court: Tape recordings. The audio on these tapes showed a Vincent Gigante that was wholly capable of speaking and thinking lucidly. Now, the prosecution did not have to rely on mafiosi witnesses. Now, they had the cold, hard proof. In his prison cell for the remaining years of his life, and after pleading guilty to ensure leniency on his family, Gigante, at long last, dropped the act. The world now knew that the bizarre behavior was an elaborate, years-long trick, and Gigante was reportedly calm, collected, and confident while in prison following his outing. In the Winter of 2005, at age 77, Vincent Gigante died while incarcerated at a prison medical center.

The Final Crackdown

During most of the period of Gigante's incarceration, Matty Ianniello served as acting boss. Between Gigante's two convictions, the Family was weakened and was ripe for exploitation. Mike D'Urso, an associate of the Family, soon turned witness. Around the same time, one of the *capo* crews was infiltrated by an undercover agent. The efforts of the two moles eventually resulted in the conviction of several Genovese captains and dozens of low-level members and associates. Now, not only was the leadership structure of the Family disrupted, but many of the foot soldiers who comprised the muscle for the organization were put away. Perhaps the highest profile of the crimes they were charged with was attempting to siphon millions of dollars out of a credit union of the *New York Times* newspaper.

For a time, Ianniello had controlled a prostitution ring in New York and had become entangled in extortion with a bus drivers' union. But, around the time of Gigante's death, Ianniello's time would also be coming to an end. In an 11 month period between 2005 and 2006, Ianniello was indicted twice, once in New York and once in Connecticut. The Connecticut charge was in regard to his involvement in extorting garbage removal contracts, a market that had become a Mafia staple in large cities. Given the fact that the acting boss' health was in dire straits, he was treated lightly in court. He pled guilty in both state-level crimes and served two years in a North Carolina federal prison, before dying at his New York residence in the Summer of 2012.

After Gigante (the official boss) had died and Ianniello had abdicated after his indictment, Daniel Leo (his real surname may be Leonetti), a former captain, became boss. It seemed as though the Genovese Family was once again coalescing around a strong leadership structure, however in reality, the Family no longer had a formidable central figure with any real longevity or notoriety. Leo was soon convicted on loansharking charges, along with several other Genovese men. He would end up only serving five years, but after being released in 2013, his position as boss was likely already occupied. This is not fully clear, however. In 2010, for the same charges Daniel Leo faced, the boss' nephew and top captain Joe Leo was also convicted. Joe had helped Daniel operate his New York gambling and loansharking rings.

Much of Leo's story is not a matter of record. It is known that he was at one point a member of East Harlem's "Purple Gang," a relatively loose collaboration of drug pushers and buttonmen. For much of its history, the gang was only loosely affiliated with Mafia structures, but eventually developed close ties with the Genoveses, especially under the reign of "The Chin" Gigante. Leo's rise was fairly meteoric, going from an unaffiliated associate to a *capo* and eventually to head of the entire organization. Regardless of his history, it is safe to say that both Daniel Leo and Joe Leo are essentially non-factors in the Mafia lore. This will be discussed more shortly.

By this point, it was clear that no one in the Mafia structure was even remotely safe. Everyone from low-level non-members up to bosses were being prosecuted. This era would see the decimation of the ranks of the Genovese Crime Family, and their position as a powerful Mafia Family has since been in question. As far as Italian-American organized crime goes, they certainly still hold sway. But, the Mafia in the present day is a shadow of its former self, an organization with seemingly no concrete adherence to old principles of *omerta* and an eagerness to flip when faced with prison time. Perhaps it was Lucky Luciano, the man known to have fully Americanized the Italian-American Mafia and put less emphasis on traditionalism, who set this trend in motion. Perhaps it was simply the pressure exerted on them from more able and willing law enforcement bodies. Regardless of the cause, the American Mafia today is simply not the illustrious, global sensation it had been decades earlier.

The Genovese Family Today

The Genovese Family today, perhaps due to the legacy and practices of Vincent Gigante, remains the most secretive and mysterious of American crime Families. Much of their current structure since the late 2000s and early 2010s is generally unclear, and it is understood that the Genoveses have taken steps to try to maintain both relevance and anonymity. During Gigante's reign, it became a necessity to reform the front boss scheme. Gigante needed someone to physically fill in for his Mafia duties while he hid himself away in his home. These individuals would become known as "street bosses," the ones who would keep their ears to the ground while the boss remained away from prying eyes.

The crackdown on organized crime, residual from the 1990s and early 2000s, continued into recent years. The Mafia's involvement in garbage disposal, among all things, would come back to haunt them yet again. The year 2013 saw another large collection of Genovese associates and enforcers charged with racketeering in the waste industry. Many simply cooperated with prosecutors, as had become the norm by this time. *Omerta* in this era was less a rule than it was an ancient legacy of nobler days. Later in the decade, more large groups would be arrested and charged, notably in a large NYPD loansharking investigation in the Fall of 2017.

Based on the record of both high-level and low-level convictions, in addition to the notable absence of anything even close to resembling a *capo di tutti capi*, the Genovese Family structure seemed irretrievably disrupted. Bosses no longer commanded mass respect as their predecessors did from the 1920s to the 1980s, and celebrities they certainly were not. One explanation seems likely: After the federal government had unleashed hell upon the Mafia, going directly for the throat of leadership through the 1980s and 1990s, many of the "old school" mafiosi, to whom *omerta* still held some semblance of meaning, even if sentimental or nostalgic, were surgically removed from the body of organized crime. The consequence of this was that many of the highest ranking positions were left vacant within a relatively short period of time. An onslaught like this was unprecedented, and the

Family ranks were not prepared. This meant that many Mafia underlings had to rush to be inserted into these vital positions, and were promoted far quicker than Mafia traditions would normally have dictated. The people now holding captain and underboss and boss positions were simply not as seasoned as their predecessors had been. Cutting their teeth in the "new school," with their would-be mentors behind bars, it seems as though many of these gangsters viewed being arrested and turning witness as a given.

Paranoia seemed to be the dominant characteristic of Mafia higher ups. As it turns out, Vincent Gigante's erratic episodes would set the tone for the future of the Genovese Family. With both the leadership and rank-and-file positions in the Mafia being less attractive than ever to prospective criminals, there was a crisis in membership. The result was a relaxation of traditional Mafia membership qualifications. Recall the early years of the Genovese Family, the years of Luciano and Masseria and the Castellammarese War. In this era, heritage-based traditionalism still held its weight, despite Luciano's willingness to work with non-Italians. In order to become Made, associates of the Family required *full* Italian heritage (sometimes, specifically Sicilian heritage, though Vito Genovese was an obvious exception). Over time this was degraded, and only the father's lineage was needed to be validated. Nowadays, given the dearth of "wannabe" gangsters, it is believed that either parent being of partially Italian heritage is enough to warrant induction into Family ranks. The quest to remain relevant has reached desperation.

The Mafia is also now less overt than ever before. Long gone are the days when mafiosi could be seen hanging around local businesses out in the open, chatting and joking with fellow respected gangsters on street corners. So-called wise guys live their lives in the shadows, with any form of notoriety being a cause for concern. Mafia-ordered hits, once a staple of both internal and external power struggles, are now rare. With modern forensic techniques and DNA profiling, Mafia Families are less free than ever to eliminate rivals with wanton disregard for legal repercussions. A devotion to strict secrecy appears to be one of the few things tethering the Genovese Family to their continued existence. It is believed that the identity of the true boss, the one calling all the shots, is kept a secret from all those except high ranking Made Genovese men. Although it is far from certain, the speculation is that a man named Liborio Bellomo is currently serving as, at least, the street boss of the Genoveses.

This culture shift within the American Mafia was extensive. The appeal of joining up with Mafia crews in the first place had been seriously tarnished. It seemed to many that eventual indictment was an inevitability, and this served as a deterrent for would-be associates. The Family's numbers dwindled and on top of that, the position of boss was less and less attractive. In previous decades, the title of boss was something to commit murder over. It was something worth scheming and plotting over. It was coveted. Today, it is likely seen as nothing but a burden and a source of paranoia. Bosses do not receive the respect that legendary leaders like Morello, Luciano, and Vito Genovese enjoyed, and Made Men could not be trusted to keep their silence. According to the famous Mob Museum in Las Vegas, Vincent Gigante was the last in the era of "celebrity" bosses. Ianniello and Leo would never become household names, nor would the successors. Some of the first words Tony utters in *The Sopranos* ring true for the general sentiment of modern day Mafia bosses: "It's good to be in something from the ground floor. I came too late for that, I know. But lately I'm getting the feeling that I came in at the end. The best is over."

Conclusion

In August of 2022, a popular coffee shop in Long Island made headlines in the *New York Times*. As it turns out, it had been functioning for almost 10 years as a front for an illegal gambling ring run by the Genovese and Bonanno Families. The coffee house was just one in a series of front businesses exposed by the years-long investigation by both federal and New York-based law enforcement. The operation had been aided with the cooperation of a 15-year veteran detective of the NYPD, who allegedly raided rival gambling operations at the request of Genovese and Bonanno leaders in exchange for payoffs.

Nine gangsters from both Families were charged, and the detective was suspended without pay on a strict zero tolerance policy toward police involvement in organized crime. Carmelo Polito, allegedly a current Genovese *capo*, has also been charged with operating illegal gambling websites and with threatening the murder of an individual who had become indebted to Polito through his gambling losses. All had been charged with racketeering as a part of an ongoing criminal organization. The other fronts investigated included a shoe repair shop and a soccer club in Queens, all of which were discovered to house secret areas for gambling. But, the coffee shop alone is estimated to have brought in around $10,000 USD every week.

What can this story, only a couple of months old at the time of writing, tell us about the current state of the Mafia? Obviously, the Five Families are still alive and well. They continue to be a factor in American organized crime, especially in the epicenter of New York City. The story also makes clear that despite the intense heat that organized crime has received since the 1980s, there is still plenty of money to be made on the wrong side of the law: Nearly a half million dollars in estimated income from *a single* gambling operation is nothing to scoff at. Clearly, there is still some incentive in operating as a mafioso.

We can also see that federal and state law enforcement have not been resting on their laurels since their RICO suits decimated the traditional Mafia leadership in prior decades. Agencies are still willing to devote years of work and massive dollar amounts to fund investigations into criminal Mafia activity. Further, we can see that there is still incentive for police to corrupt themselves under the influence of mafiosi. This, of course, has always been the case, but something about the detective's punishment gives us a hint as to how things have changed. Typically, instant punishment for the wrongdoings of police officers are rare. Even rarer is withholding pay from officers who have been suspended. In this case, the state of New York sent a clear message to anyone in law enforcement willing to sell their services to criminal groups. None of this should be surprising—New York City has seen the effects of unfettered organized crime and rampant police corruption in service of those crimes. The fact that the federal and state agencies maintain a hardline stance toward the Mafia, even as late as 2022, does not bode well for the future of this Sicilian-American subculture which made its debut in the United States well over a century ago.

However, one thing should be clear by the conclusion of this book: The Mafia is inherently opportunistic, secretive, and dreadfully persistent. After all this time and decades of persecution, it is unlikely that the Mafia will die out any time soon. What is more likely is that the Five Families and their affiliates will continue to operate in the shadows, on the margins of society, far away from the limelight that past celebrity bosses, like Genovese and Luciano, had enjoyed. The Mafia, like most organizations, should be seen as an organic, living thing. It adapts or it dies, and throughout its history, the Mafia has been proven to be highly adaptable.

The Genovese Family, an organization founded by Sicilian mafioso Giuseppe Morello and named after Neapolitan don Vito Genovese, remains today one of the most powerful and esoteric criminal organizations in the United States. From the early days of the 1890s, through the tumultuous war torn years of the 1910s, prohibition and bloody war in the 1920s and 1930s, consolidation in the 1940s and 1950s, internal betrayal in the 1960s, to intense persecution in the 1980s and 1990s, the Genoveses have weathered an incredible storm. The crusades led by Thomas Dewey, Orange Dickie, Robert Kennedy,

J. Edgar Hoover, and Rudy Giuliani, among others, have made immense strides in incapacitating criminal organizations, yet in the light of such recent news stories, we must be frank: They were failures.

Though many now believe that the Mafia exists only as a remnant of wilder, more lawless days, only to be rediscovered in nostalgic films like *The Godfather* or *Goodfellas* or *Donnie Brasco*, some significant portion of crime in North America is still monopolized by *La Cosa Nostra*. Given the fact that it took decades for the existence of the Mafia to even become a matter of public record, perhaps it is something that will never go away, even when we have convinced ourselves it has. Perhaps it will remain a factor in organized crime forever. Perhaps what is needed, before the final death knell of the Mafia is rang, is yet another young, ambitious crusader.

References

Catanzaro, R. (1986). The mafia. *Italian Politics,* (1), 87-101. https://www.jstor.org/stable/43039574

Catino, M. (2014). How do mafias organize? *European Journal of Sociology, 55*(2), 177–220. https://doi.org/10.1017/s0003975614000095

Closson, T. (2022, August 16). Two of New York's Oldest Mafia Clans Charged in Money Laundering Scheme. *The New York Times.* https://www.nytimes.com/2022/08/16/nyregion/new-york-mob-families-racketeering-charges.html

Cohen, S. (2009, March 8). It's a mob family circus. *New York Post.* https://nypost.com/2009/03/08/its-a-mob-family-circus/

DeStefano, A. M. (2021). *The deadly don: Vito Genovese, mafia boss.* Citadel Press.

Finckenauer, J. O. (2012). *Mafia and Organized Crime.* Simon and Schuster.

Former acting boss of Genovese crime family sentenced in Manhattan federal court to 18 additional months in prison. (2010). United States Attorney Southern District of New York. https://www.justice.gov/archive/usao/nys/pressreleases/March10/leodanielsentencingpr.pdf

Gosch, M. A., & Hammer, R. (2013). *The last testament of Lucky Luciano : The mafia story in his own words.* Enigma Books.

Jacobs, J. B., & Gouldin, L. P. (1999). Cosa Nostra: The final chapter? *Crime and Justice, 25,* 129–189. https://doi.org/10.1086/449288

Jacobs, J. B., & Peters, E. (2003). Labor racketeering: The mafia and the unions. *Crime and Justice, 30,* 229–282. https://www.jstor.org/stable/1147700

JFK Assassination Records - Findings. (2016, August 15). National Archives. https://www.archives.gov/research/jfk/select-committee-report/part-1c.html

Miller, W. (Ed.). (2022). *Vito Genovese*. Sage. https://sk-sagepub-com.ledproxy2.uwindsor.ca/reference/socialhistory-crime-punishment/n267.xml

Muller, M. (2005, July 28). *Reputed Genovese family members indicted - Jul 28, 2005*. www.cnn.com; CNN. https://www.cnn.com/2005/LAW/07/28/mafia.racketeering/index.html

Powell, H. (2015). *Lucky Luciano : the man who organized crime in America*. Barricade Books Inc.

Racketeer Influenced and Corrupt Organizations Act (RICO). (2011, October 10). www.nolo.com; Nolo. https://www.nolo.com/legal-encyclopedia/content/rico-act.html

Rubinsky, C. (2007, May 9). *Reputed mob boss sentenced in trash case*. www.washingtonpost.com. https://www.washingtonpost.com/wp-dyn/content/article/2006/06/09/AR2006060900500.html

Raab, S. (2005). *Five families: The rise, decline, and resurgence of America's most powerful Mafia empires*. St. Martin's Press.

Schellie, P. D. (1985). Racketeer influenced and corrupt organizations act. *The Business Lawyer*, *40*, (3), 1133-1137. https://www.jstor.org/stable/40686656

The Mob Museum. https://themobmuseum.org/

Printed in Great Britain
by Amazon